What to Do When You're Dating a Jew

Everything You Need to Know from Matzah Balls to Marriage

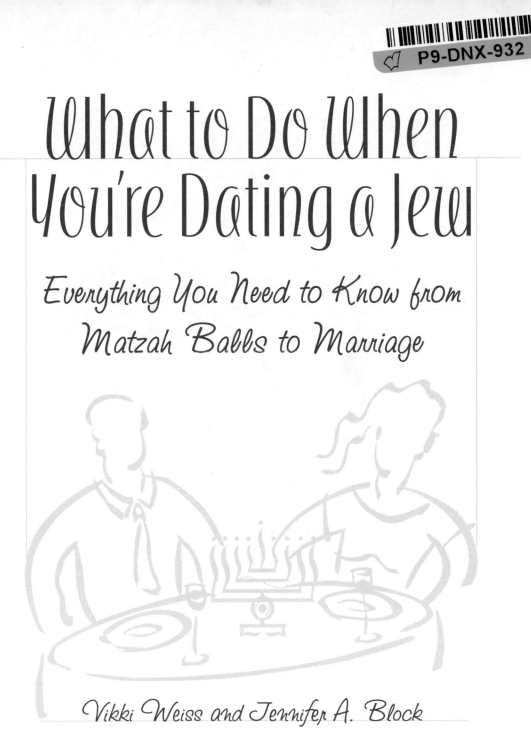

Vikki Weiss and Jennifer A. Block

THREE RIVERS PRESS • NEW YORK

Published by Three Rivers Press, New York, New York. Member of the Crown Publishing Group.

Random House, Inc. New York, Toronto, London, Sydney, Auckland

www.randomhouse.com

THREE RIVERS PRESS is a registered trademark and the Three Rivers Press colophon is a trademark of Random House, Inc.

Designed by Lauren Dong and Sue Maksuta

Printed in the United States of America

Library of Congress Cataloging-in-Publication Data
Weiss, Vikki.
    What to do when you're dating a Jew : everything you need to know from matzah balls to marriage / by Vikki Weiss and Jennifer A. Block.
        p. cm.
    1. Interfaith marriage. 2. Judaism—Customs and practices. 3. Courtship—Religious aspects—Judaism. 4. Jews—United States—Social life and customs. I. Block, Jennifer A. II. Title.
HQ1031.W45 2000
306.84'3—dc21   00-037723

ISBN 0-609-80639-4

10 9 8 7 6 5 4 3 2 1

First Edition

What to Do When You're Dating a Jew

Everything You Need to Know from Matzah Balls to Marriage

To Laurie Rosenow, my closest friend and a shiksa who really knows how to noodge. Had it not been for her weekly proddings ("Are you working on the book? You've got to write the book. It's going to be a best-seller!"), this book would never have come to fruition.

—Vikki

To my parents, Michael and Judith Block, for respecting my decision to marry someone outside the faith. To my husband, Dave Martin, for welcoming my crazy, wonderful Jewish family with open arms. And in memory of Ruth A. Mass and Anna Block, who would have been so proud of their bubeleh.

—Jennifer

Contents

Acknowledgments

First, we'd like to thank our mothers for raising us to be nice Jewish girls with a sense of humor. Vikki's mom, Suzanne Weiss, will get extra Hanukkah gelt this year for writing the introduction and acting as our editor before we were lucky enough to land Sarah Silbert at Three Rivers Press. And we can't thank our agent, Linda Konner, enough for championing this project from the beginning.

The rest of our family members deserve credit as well. Without the love, encouragement, and support (in the form of a Toshiba laptop) given by Ben and Maureen Weiss, Vikki would have never had the courage or the means to take two months off and write in Lake Tahoe. Without Lisa Weiss's laser printer and secretary, the manuscript would have never been delivered on time. Lisa also served as an excellent content consultant. Thanks to Eric and Ellyn Weiss and their spouses (Keni Renner and Leo Schmitz), who inspired the book.

Many thanks to Elizabeth Block and Eric Block (for sharing a lifetime of fun family memories), Lisa Friedman (for the recipes), and Jennifer's parents' friends (for enthusiastically spreading the word about *What to Do When . . .*).

Thanks to all of our rabbis, maggids, Saturday, Sunday, and Hebrew school teachers, and camp counselors across the country who helped us become the Jews that we are today.

Finally, thanks to all of our friends who have laughed at our jokes, told us great stories, tested recipes, and patiently listened to us talk about *The Book* for over a year. We love you all.

—Vikki and Jennifer

Preface

Megan Kelly first met the Greensteins, her future in-laws, at a kosher deli. She ordered a ham and cheese sandwich. She needs this book. She is not alone. According to a 1990 national Jewish population study, a staggering 52 percent of American Jews marry someone outside their faith. And that leaves a lot of room for slip-ups like Megan's. We've been there, and we're here to help you survive mealtimes, holidays, and shopping excursions with Jewish family and friends.

What to Do When You're Dating a Jew: Everything You Need to Know from Matzah Balls to Marriage will introduce you to all things Jewish, from chicken soup to "Seinfeld," from Hanukkah *gelt* to "*oy gevalt!*" With your newfound knowledge, you'll feel confident drinking your four cups of wine at the Passover *seder* table. You'll trade Yiddish barbs with the best of them. You'll be leading the *hora* at the next wedding. Heck, you could even whip up a *Shabbat* dinner from scratch.

As Jewish women, we have a lifetime of experience dealing with Jewish men and their families. We're happy to enlighten those in need of a little guidance. You don't have to thank us. Just the fact that you have this book in your hands gives our mothers great *naches.**

Enjoy!

—Vikki Weiss and Jennifer A. Block
January 6, 2000

---

* Joy parents derive from their children

What to Do When You're Dating a Jew

Everything You Need to Know from Matzah Balls to Marriage

Introduction

By Suzanne Weiss,
Vikki Weiss's mom

Let's begin at the beginning.

When I was a young bride, standing under the *chuppah* (the Jewish bridal canopy, symbolizing, among other things, the future home the couple will build), the rabbi (oh, come on, you know what a rabbi is) exhorted me to be a good Jewish wife: to light candles on the Sabbath, to observe the holy days, and to bring up my children in the Jewish faith. All of which I did.

Yet in spite of the fact that I followed all of the rules —or perhaps because of it—my children (including one of the authors of this book) have presented me with a succession of non-Jewish in-laws . . . and they're still coming. Over the years, my children's spouses became my children as well. By the way, the rabbi who literally put the fear of God into me on that long-ago wedding day wasn't spared the changing times either. He lived long enough to welcome an African-American in-law into his own family.

I still keep a Jewish home, to the occasional bemusement of my non-Jewish children-in-law. They have had to learn to eat *latkes* (potato pancakes) on Hanukkah and participate in the Passover *seder*. It hasn't always been easy, but to our credit, we all keep trying. If they ever get around to giving me grandchildren, I'm sure the complications will multiply. And I'm just as sure that we will deal with them.

In the old days, in the Eastern European *shtetls* (think *Fiddler on the Roof*) to which most American Jews can trace their roots, life was easier. All you had to worry about was scratching out a living and running away from the cossacks. Assimilation was out of the question.

When my great-grandmother Judith—my *bubbe*—came to this country, she brought with her little besides her heavy brass Sabbath candlesticks and some five thousand years of tradition. My grandmother passed these along to me, along with the family recipe for chicken soup and some nice shares of AT&T—before it started splitting.

I sold the stock but I still have the candlesticks, which I hope one of my daughters will inherit and use. Plus I have the recipe, practically guaranteed to cure everything from mild depression to menstrual cramps to the common cold, which I will share with you. What else can a Jewish mother do?

MOM'S CHICKEN SOUP

> *1 stewing hen, cleaned and quartered*
> *Several teaspoons salt (keep tasting, I never seem to add enough)*
> *4–6 carrots, peeled*
> *4–6 large stalks of celery, cut up*
> *2 large onions, peeled and halved*
> *Small bunch of parsley*

Schmaltz, or chicken fat, was considered a delicacy in the old days and used in making chopped liver or spread like butter on bread. No wonder so many of my uncles expired from heart attacks!

In a stock pot, cover chicken with water, add salt, and bring to a boil. With slotted spoon, skim off the film that forms at top of the pot (use a clean paper towel to clean the rim). Reduce heat and cover. Peel and cut up the vegetables and add to the pot after skimming again, if necessary. It is not a bad idea to add more salt at this point as well. Simmer for three hours. Cool and strain. (Strip chicken from bones to use in chicken salad or casseroles; slice carrots to float in soup if desired, but store separately.) Refrigerate liquid until fat forms a solid crust at the top of the container. It can easily be lifted off at this point and discarded. Reheat soup and serve with wide egg noodles or *matzah* balls and plenty of love.

First Things First:
The Basics of Judaism

WHY YOU NEED THIS BOOK

So *you're dating someone Jewish.* Or maybe you've already married that someone. Well, you've come to the right place. This book will enlighten you to all things Jewish, from *knishes* to *kreplach*, kosher to *keppe.**

It is a quick reference guide to help you feel comfortable in Jewish circles. It is not a resource for all things Jewish. It is not meant to tell anyone how to be a Jew, nor is it a guide to conversion, God forbid. All we're trying to do is to keep you from ordering a ham and cheese sandwich in a kosher deli or planning a party to celebrate the Jewish New Year. Think of it as a little advance warning about what you are getting into by dating a Jew. You'll thank us later.

You may even surprise your loved one with your newfound knowledge. More important, you'll be more at ease in situations that could otherwise be awkward because of cultural differences. You'll know what to expect, what to do, and what to say. And it's a good

CULTURAL JEWS

People who are Jewish by birth consider themselves to be Jewish and identify with the Jewish culture even though they do not regularly practice the religious rituals and traditions. These individuals might also refer to themselves as "ethnic Jews."

---

*Knishes are large dumplings filled with potato, minced meat, or spinach; kreplach are dumplings with chopped meat or cheese usually in soup (think puffy wontons); kosher means "fit to eat" in Hebrew; keppe means head.

PROSELYTIZE THIS

Jews do not openly proselytize. No one is going to come knocking at your door. In fact, rabbis discourage non-Jews who want to convert until the rabbis are convinced they are sincere and want to convert for the right reasons (monotheism, devotion to the Torah, etc.). The vast majority of converts are non-Jewish women who marry Jewish men. They usually convert so their children will be born Jewish. However, if you are involved with a Reform Jew, this is no longer necessary. In the 1980s the Union of American Hebrew Congregations, the major association of Reform congregations, decided that if one parent is Jewish, the child is Jewish. How nice, easy, and Reform.

thing, because, like the old Hebrew proverb says, "A slip of the foot is better than a slip of the tongue."

Why Are So Many Jewish Parents Opposed to Interfaith Dating?

Jews think of themselves as a separate people—this is a reason in itself. But it also ties in with the sad fact that Jewish populations are plummeting. Judaism, one of the oldest organized religions in the world, is in great danger of dying out. Jewish birth rates are pretty low to begin with. Then there's the fact that one third of the world's Jewish population perished in the Holocaust. With interfaith marriage, this population depletion continues. Even before we had these statistics to worry about, Jews grieved when a child married out of the faith. Pogroms and holocausts aside, Jewish life is rich and beautiful. Practicing Jews don't want their kids to miss out on that. If your mate's parents aren't practicing, you should have a much easier time of it.

THE BASICS

Anyone who tells you "the reason for this is . . ." is wrong. There is more than one reason for everything in Judaism. In fact, there are 600,000 reasons for everything, according to the *Zohar**. But that doesn't stop most Jews from being know-it-alls.

THE CHOSEN PEOPLE

It's a mystery why God chose the Jews. In fact, Jews often ask God "Why us?" Looking at the history of the Judaism, one might assume a "light unto the nations" means a light for oppressive rulers and crazy mobs to try to extinguish. This is not so. That God called Jews a "light unto the nations" means that Jews are supposed to lead exemplary, moral lives and set an example for other people. In

---

*The *Zohar* is the central text of the *cabala*, ancient Jewish mysticism. While most Jews don't study the cabala, any rabbi will tell you that most rituals have many meanings.

return, God will watch over the Jews and give them the land of Israel. This is the deal, the covenant. It is, however, not as easy as it sounds. Observant Jews work extremely hard to live the kind of life God wanted them to live. Sometimes they've got to wonder if it's such an honor. It's like being president of the temple. It sounds good, it looks easy, but oy, it's a job you'd wish on your worst enemy.

GOD

Jews believe in one huge God. God is everywhere. God knows everything. God can do anything. That's about all we know. It's very hush-hush. Jewish theologians sometimes say that it is easier to describe God by what God is not than by what God is. Jews aren't even supposed to know the name of God. Nor are we supposed to write out the alias: G-o-d. That is why you might come across some Jewish writings and see God spelled "G-d." Apparently, if the "o" is omitted no sin has been committed.

In the same vein, Jews do not begin to imagine what God looks like. According to the book of Exodus, God says, "You cannot see my face. For no man can see me and live." God is supposed to create a sense of mystery and wonder rather than be the provider of neat solutions.

An important theme in Judaism is that God is dependent upon man when wanting to act in the world. This means that God's presence is inextricably bound with people. The Lord is passionately involved with the affairs of mankind. In fact, the Jewish idea is to foster a sense of God within each person so that dealings with others are viewed as sacred encounters.

FREE WILL

Even though God already knows everything that is going to happen to man, Judaism maintains that people have freedom of choice. In some ways, this seems like a paradox. Think of it this way, just because God knows what is going to happen does not mean that man doesn't get to choose whether he is going to be sinful or ethical.

THE MOST IMPORTANT PRAYER IN JUDAISM

The *Sh'ma* is the Jewish affirmation of faith, recited in the morning and before going to bed. Jews are also supposed to say the Sh'ma as their last words before dying: "Hear O Israel, the Lord is our God. The Lord is one. Blessed is his glorious kingdom forever and ever."

THE GOLDEN RULE OF JUDAISM

If I am not for myself, who will be for me?

And if I am only for myself, what am I?

And if not now, when?

––––
Rabbi Hillel, *Ethics of the Fathers* 1:14

● ● ● ● ● ● ● ● ● ● ● ● ● ● ● ● ● ● ●

ORIGINAL SIN

Judaism believes that people are born with a clean slate. The sin bank is empty. Unfortunately, this could be a temporary situation. Born with opposing life forces, one pulling a person to do good and the other to do evil, everyone at one time or another will be inclined to do evil. Whether they do or not is up to them. To make it easier to do good, God gave the Jews the Torah, a text teeming with tips on how to lead a good life. With vivid descriptions of the horrible fates that befall sinners—turning into a pillar of salt, drowning in a flood, being tormented by plagues—the Torah also makes a pretty poor case for sinning. The good news for sinners is that when someone does sin, as humans are apt to do, he can redeem himself through repentance and good deeds.

DUALITY

Someone who loves God and follows all the ritual commandments but isn't compassionate toward his fellow man is not cutting it as a Jew. Praying is half of it. Love for other people, usually manifested by good works or *gemilut hasidim* (acts of loving kindness), is the rest of it.

THE MESSIAH

Jews believe in the eventual coming of the Messiah. However, it hasn't happened yet. The Jews are still waiting. According to Jewish teachings, a descendant of the house of David will come and redeem humanity and establish the reign of God on earth. Most Jews today think of the Messiah as humanity collectively rather than as an individual savior, so people can usher in the Messianic Age by their own actions of kindness, justice, and enlightenment. In fact, Jews believe that the fate of the world depends upon man bringing in the Messiah through right action. Every commandment performed tips the scales in favor of redemption. Conversely, every unjust action is a setback. Therefore, according to the Jew, if one person does something bad, he tips the scales against himself and the entire world. This must be where Jewish guilt originated.

Many Christians are curious as to Jesus Christ's place in Judaism. Jews do not deny the existence of Jesus Christ, but do not believe he is the Messiah. In fact, they don't really think about him at all. To Jews, Jesus was a person. He was a teacher. He was a Jew. Judaism had been around a long time before he came on the scene. If we thought he was holy, we'd be Christians, right? And once and for all, the Jews did not kill Jesus. The Romans did.

THE REST OF THE WORLD

One reason why you need this book is that Jews have their own language. Several of them, actually. Even American-born, English-speaking Jews pepper their speech with snippets of Hebrew and Yiddish. One language just isn't enough to supply the endless streams of chatter. Yiddish in particular adds some descriptive words.

What would you do if you heard yourself referred to as a *shiksa* or a *shaygets*? Don't panic or get angry. If you are a woman and you're not Jewish, you're a shiksa. Shiksa is simply the term for a non-Jewish woman. Lesser used is shaygets, a non-Jewish male. A *goy*, which literally means "stranger," is anyone who is not Jewish. For example: "My son with the shiksa. No one settles down with a nice Jewish girl anymore."

DIFFERENT TYPES OF JUDAISM

Jews categorize themselves by level and type of observance. The main movements are Orthodox, Conservative, and Reform. The modern Reconstructionist movement is also gaining popularity. There are other movements, but for the sake of simplicity, this book only mentions the most established and mainstream of them.

ORTHODOX

This is the strictest, most to-the-letter form of Judaism. Like the Catholic Church, Jewish Orthodoxy has been criticized for not adapting the rules to better fit contemporary life. You can usually recog-

WHAT IS A JEW?

A race? A nation? A religion? People identify with Judaism on many levels: historically, culturally, spiritually. There is no real definition of being Jewish. Jews are an extremely complex group of people. The Israeli parliament has changed the definition of being a Jew three times in the past fifty years. It is hard to combine spiritual, cultural, and religious identities. This we do know: The Jews started off as a family. All Jews are descendants of Abraham and the tribal house of Israel. However, blood is not vital to Judaism. Belief in one God and the Torah is what counts. The nation of Israel came to be long before it ever had any land. Israel, the Holy Land, is historic fulfillment for the Jews, but not their origin.

SHIKSA

The bad news is it's the Hebrew word for "blemish." The good news is that modern Hebrew and Yiddish dictionaries define it as "a pretty, non-Jewish young woman." As Philip Roth wrote, "It may have been gold in the streets to my grandparents, it may have been a chicken in every pot to my father and mother, but to me . . . America is a *shiksa* nestling under your arm whispering love love love love love!"

. . . .

nize Orthodox Jews by the way they dress. Men always wear *yarmulkes* (skullcaps) or hats, and married women always cover their heads, usually with a wig. The men cover their heads as a sign of respect to God. Women wear wigs or hats because the Talmud says that a religious woman should cover her hair so as not to inspire lust in men. Orthodox men often wear beards, thereby heeding the commandment that says you shall not "destroy the corners of your beard." Today, Orthodox Jews are allowed to use electric razors but not a straight-edge blade. Ultra Orthodox men also wear long side curls called *payos* (pronounced "pay-us").

Orthodox men and boys over the age of thirteen also wear *tefillin* (pronounced "te-fill-in"), two black leather cubes with long leather straps, during daily morning prayer. The cubes contain passages from the Torah written on strips of parchment. One cube is placed on the left arm facing the heart *(Shel Yad)*. The other is worn on the center of the forehead *(Shel Rosh)*. The long strap worn on the box on the arm is wrapped seven times around the arm. The strap of the forehead box is looped to allow the adjustment of the cube. Wearing tefillin is a reminder that the Torah must be read and studied every day.

The Orthodox talk a lot during their services, which usually last several hours. When they are that lengthy, who can blame them? No one minds the talking, although occasionally it will get so loud that the rabbi will stop the service to get everyone to calm down.

If you ever attend a service at an Orthodox temple, you'll notice the extreme rapidity with which the worshipers pray. They actually are in a hurry—not to get out of temple, but to fit in as many prayers as possible. Through the years, as more and more prayers were written, they were added to the prayer book. Soon, there were so many prayers, there wasn't enough time to get through them all. Despite all the rushing, Orthodox services are still very long. That's why people are always going in and out during the service. Sometimes you just need to take a break.

HASIDISM

The Hasidic movement came about during the spiritual and economic depression resulting from the cossack massacres in Eastern

Europe in the seventeenth century. By the early twentieth century, it affected half of world Jewry. It is much less popular now. Hasidic Jews believe that sincere devotion, zeal, and heartfelt prayers are more acceptable to God than great learning, that God is best served through deep-seated joy rather than intellectualism and solemnity.

At its inception, the Orthodox majority was shocked by Hasidism. Yet it offered an alternative for many Jews who did not want to cope with the complex and detailed learning of the *yeshivas* (Jewish schools). People were ready to accept the mystic teachings of the Baal Shem Tov, father of the Hasidic movement, in order to feel new hope and become closer to God. Like the Orthodox, Hasidic men wear black hats, beards, and payos and married women wear dresses and wigs.

CONSERVATIVE

In the nineteenth century, Zechariah Frankel wanted to change Judaism but wanted to do it gradually and minimally. Conservative Jews are still quite religious but much less strict on lifestyle issues. Conservatism is also known as the "middle way."

REFORM

Reform Jews are the least religious and observant of Jewish law. Reform Judaism began in Germany in the early nineteenth century. While it never took off in Germany, it has huge appeal in America, where the vast majority of Jews today are Reform. Orthodox Jews in Israel do not recognize Reform Jews as being Jewish—a point of contention among the Jewish people.

RECONSTRUCTIONIST

The first American movement, Reconstructionism is based on the principles and theories of New York's Rabbi Mordecai M. Kaplan. Reconstructionists see Judaism as a "religious civilization" rather than exclusively a religion. They believe that Judaism must undergo constant change and development to meet the needs of modern con-

JEWISH VERSUS GOYISH

"If you live in New York or any other big city, you are Jewish. It doesn't matter even if you're Catholic; if you live in New York, you're Jewish. If you live in Butte, Montana, you're going to be goyish *even if you're Jewish.*

"Kool-Aid is goyish. Evaporated milk is goyish (even if the Jews invented it). Chocolate is Jewish and fudge is goyish. Fruit salad is Jewish. Lime Jell-O is goyish. Lime soda is very goyish. Trailer parks are so goyish that Jews won't go near them."

—LENNY BRUCE

A young Jewish student left Poland for America and returned many years later to visit his mother.

"Sheldon, where is your beard?" asks his mother.

"Mama, in America nobody wears a beard."

"But at least you keep the Sabbath?"

"Mama, business is business. In America people work on the Sabbath."

"But kosher food you still eat?"

"Mama, it's very hard to keep kosher in America."

The old woman hesitates for a moment and in a coarse whisper she says, "Sheldon, tell me one thing. Are you still circumcised?"

ditions. They say that Jewish life in America needs to be "reconstructed" to allow the modern Jew to be fully satisfied with his association with the Jewish people. The Reconstructionist movement does not focus on the supernatural at all.

You might also hear Jews referring to themselves as Ashkenazic or Sephardic. This has to do with what area of the world their family comes from. Ashkenazic Jews are from Eastern and Western European countries and Scandinavia. Sephardic Jews hail from Spanish, the Mediterranean, and Arab countries. Ashkenazic and Sephardic Jews vary in culture, ritual, social customs, and the pronunciation of Hebrew words. Sephardic Jews have their own language, Ladino, which combines Hebrew and Spanish, just as Yiddish combines Hebrew and German. Like Yiddish, Ladino has suffered a serious decline in recent generations.

JEWISH CLERGY

There are two main players in Jewish services: the rabbi and the cantor. The rabbi, which means "teacher" in Hebrew, leads the services and is also available for counseling. Yes, rabbis can marry and have children. Women can be ordained as rabbis in the Reform temple, and some reform rabbis will perform interfaith marriages. If you're engaged, you'll probably meet with the rabbi several times to plan your wedding ceremony.

The cantor is like the rabbi's singing sidekick. He helps lead the service and does most of the requisite singing and chanting. If you want to learn more about cantors, rent the remake of the movie *The Jazz Singer*. No one sings the Kol Nidre prayer like Neil Diamond.

BROTHER BRONSTEIN? SISTER SCHWARTZ?

When was the last time you saw a Jewish monk? How about a nun? If you've ever seen one, you're *meshuggener*—"crazy" in Yiddish. There's no such thing. Withdrawing from the community, as monks and nuns do at least to a certain degree, goes against the Jewish tradition. It's a good thing because, generally speaking, Jews wouldn't be at all good with the self-deprivation monks need to do. Vows of silence? Celibacy? Please! Jews believe that people who fully participate in the life around them best achieve holiness. Help the sick, feed the poor, support the fallen but do so while you raise a family, for God's sake.

WHERE JEWS PRAY

Shul is the Yiddish word for house of prayer. Synagogue and temple are synonyms. Orthodox Jews usually use the word *shul*. Conservative Jews say they are going to synagogue. Reform Jews go to temple, but not often.

The synagogue concept dates back more than two thousand years. A synagogue serves three purposes: a house of worship, a place of assembly, and a center of study.

Like Jews, temples identify themselves by level of observance such as Orthodox, Conservative, and Reform. There are no icons or idols because one of the Ten Commandments says "Thou shalt not make unto thee any graven image." The blessing over the wine means we are blessing the fruit of the earth. When blessing bread, we are actually thanking God for food.

But be prepared: There is one thing that Jewish services aren't— and that's short. Rosh Hashanah and Yom Kippur services can be as long as four hours even in Reform temples. Conservative and Orthodox worshipers stay all day. Penny Rosenow, an Illinois teacher, found that out the hard way. "One of my students invited me to his *bar mitzvah*. I arrived a polite, Protestant half hour early. I was amazed to see others arrive half an hour into the ceremony, even more appalled to see people arrive about an hour late. By the conclusion of the ceremony, hours later, I realized that the late arrivals were merely experienced Jews and other smart people."

You and your significant other should discuss whether you will join him or her at temple. Shoshana's husband went a few times but was confused by all the Hebrew. He prefers family dinners and home-centered holidays. Cynthia, however, enjoys going to temple with her Jewish husband because she's enthralled by the spirituality and age-old rituals.

RABBI

Rebbe (Yiddish); *Rav* (Hebrew)
1. teacher (literal). 2. Jewish religious and spiritual leader (modern).

CANTOR

Chazzen or *hazzan* (Hebrew)
1. Official who leads the congregation in prayer.
2. The singer/song leader.

TORAH CLIFF NOTES

One day, a heathen came to see the great Rabbi Hillel and challenged him to explain the whole Torah while he stood on one foot. Hillel said, "What is hateful to you, do not do to your neighbor. This is the whole Torah; the rest is commentary. Now go and study."*

Some say that Jesus learned the Golden Rule—Do unto others as you would have others do unto you—from Hillel.

_____

*Babylonian Talmud, *Shabbat* 31a

. . . .

Seating at temple is first come, first served, so park it where you can. Temples generally do not have family pews. The only restriction to seating arrangements occurs in Orthodox temples, where men and women sit separately.

THE MINYAN

Technically, Jews are supposed to pray three times a day. Those who don't have to haul it back and forth to the temple all day long. Since Jews can pray alone, they will most likely say their morning prayers at home before going to work. However, Judaism regards communal, public prayer as a higher form of worship than private prayer.

A minimum of ten bar mitzvah'd Jewish males over the age of thirteen is necessary for community worship, reciting the Kaddish (mourner's prayer), and for reading the Torah. This required group is called a *minyan,* which is the Hebrew word for number. The concept of needing a minyan for public worship originated from a biblical injunction in which the Israelites were divided into ten-family units to facilitate government and administration. Some movements of Judaism are beginning to allow women to be counted in the minyan, although that is quite rare. According to Jewish law, women are not required to pray, as is the case with men. As the woman is responsible for the home and raising the children, she is bound by very few of the time-sensitive commandments. Praying three times a day is one such commandment that the woman traditionally forgoes.

THE TEXTS

THE TORAH

The most important thing inside a temple is the Torah. Almost everything we know about Judaism comes from this book, which is said to be the word of God dictated to Moses on Mount Sinai. The overriding principle of Judaism is right conduct toward other people. The Torah lays out a blueprint for this conduct. Every temple must have at least one Torah.

Most non-Jews know the Torah as the Old Testament. Since Jews do not believe in the New Testament, we don't use this term. You'll also hear it called the Bible or the Five Books of Moses. These books are further divided into Torah portions. One portion is read each Saturday morning as well as on Mondays, Thursdays, and for special festivals and holidays. This way, it takes exactly one year to read the entire thing.

In the broader sense, Torah applies to all the teachings, laws, philosophies, and customs of Judaism. Therefore, although the Torah itself is a finite text, Torah study can go on indefinitely. The Torah is constantly being interpreted and reinterpreted.

Judaism promotes questioning, arguing, and interpretation. The tradition encourages people to form their own opinions and speak out for what they believe in. It also means that there are a lot of interpretations and points of view. Ask four Jews a question and you'll get five opinions.

THE TALMUD

The name Talmud has been applied to the text that, next to the Torah, is considered the second greatest literary achievement of the Jewish people. The Talmud is interpretation and commentary on the Torah. The massive text is comprised of two parts, the Mishnah and the Gemara. The Mishnah, edited in C.E. 220, is the oldest code of Jewish law. It is made up of vast amounts of material that had been orally transmitted over a span of hundreds of years. The Mishnah gives final decisions in matters of biblical interpretation. The Gemara encompasses everything the commentators had to say on a given point. If the Mishnah were to be viewed like the Bill of Rights, the Gemara would be like the Federalist papers. The Talmud is the recognized source of Jewish knowledge. For centuries, it influenced every aspect of Jewish life.

WHY TEMPLE DUES ARE SO HIGH

Physically, the Torah is big. So big that one person could throw out his back lifting it. So two people are always called upon to lift it out of

"Judaism must be probed, studied, questioned and challenged, for, in the struggle, it comes to life."

—ARI L. GOLDMAN,
THE SEARCH FOR GOD AT HARVARD

WHY ARE THERE SO MANY JEWISH LAWYERS?

It is part of the Jewish tradition. According to the Torah, to be a Jew means to continually study the Torah, which is essentially a book of Jewish law. To this point, traditional synagogue architecture calls for study tables in the main area of the temple. The rabbi is supposed to study and learn along with his students or congregation.

You might have noticed that Jews are always trying to work out a deal. God started it. On Mount Sinai, God renewed his earlier agreement with Abraham and extended it to the entire Jewish people. The deal was that God would always watch over the Jewish people. In return, they would uphold the Ten Commandments and expand them and the Torah into a code of living for all times.

SUREFIRE DIET

Whoever drops a Torah scroll has to fast for forty days.

the Ark (the cabinet where it is stored). These handmade scrolls are extremely expensive and labor intensive. The text is written in very ornate Hebrew calligraphy with a quill pen and India ink onto sheets of parchment. If the scribe, or *sofer*, makes a mistake, he has to throw the whole page away. The completed sections are sewn together with a wooden needle and thread made of animal sinew. There are sixty-two sheets or sections in all. Finally, it's rolled into two big scrolls.

Inscribing a Torah takes about a year from beginning to end, including the time it takes to check it for accuracy. They sell for $25,000 to $38,000, depending on the intricacy of the script. The high price and import of the teachings in the Torah merit the fancy duds temples dress them in. When a Torah is rolled up, there is always a velvet cover over it. Beautiful, embellished crowns symbolizing the supremacy of the Torah in all aspects of life top each scroll. Periodically, the rabbi will walk around the congregation with the dressed Torah scroll before putting it back in the Ark. People show their respect for the Torah and its teachings by touching their prayer books and *tallis* (prayer shawl) to it then kissing it.

A TOUR OF THE HOUSE

Once inside the temple, here are a few things you should know about the building:

✿ The room inside the temple where services take place is called the sanctuary. In an Orthodox sanctuary, men and women are separated. The theory behind this is that men will not keep their minds on praying if they are distracted by the presence of women. Usually, the women sit in the balcony and the men sit on the main level. Yes, it's sexist. Welcome to the world's oldest organized religion.

✿ The elevated platform where the rabbi and cantor stand is called the *bimah*. It is a big honor for a member of the congregation to be called to the bimah to read from the Torah, say a prayer, or be blessed by the rabbi.

✿ The ornate cabinet in which the Torah is kept is called the Ark. It is the holiest part of the temple because it houses the Torah and it is a reminder of the ancient Temple in Jerusalem. Renditions of the two tablets of the Ten Commandments sometimes hang above the Ark. Each time the Ark is opened, the congregation rises. The Ark should be on the eastern wall of the synagogue, the direction of Jerusalem. Jews have always faced East when praying to represent the constant prayers for the restoration of Jerusalem and Israel. In Australia, New Zealand, and India, they face West because that is the direction of Jerusalem on that side of the world. The water also goes down the drain the opposite way, but that's a different story.

✡ The lamp in front of the Ark is called the Eternal Light. It symbolizes the eminence of God and reverence for the Torah. It is also a reminder of the ancient temple and the Jewish people's eternal faith in the Jewish religion.

The Deal with the Beanies

You'll notice Jewish men putting on small caps, called yarmulkes (pronounced "yah-mah-kahs"), before entering a temple. Also called *kepot* (pronounced "key-pote") from the Hebrew word for head, these skullcaps are worn during religious events. There is no law saying people must cover their heads when in a house of prayer. It is more a point of religious etiquette. Man shows his respect to God by covering his head. Orthodox men and married women keep their heads covered at all times. Besides showing respect to God, yarmulkes help hide bald spots. Usually there's a bin near the door of the temple filled with yarmulkes. Some men have their own beautifully embroidered caps, sometimes with their Hebrew names on them, which they bobby pin in place. Many a Jewish man has found extra yarmulkes from past bar mitzvahs and weddings stuffed in his suit pocket.

Nice Scarf! Where Can I Get One?

The white fringed scarves men (and more and more women) wear in shul are called *tallis* which means prayer shawl in Hebrew. Made of silk or wool, the tallis is traditionally donned by bar mitzvah'd men during morning services and on Yom Kippur. The strings on the corners

THE TEMPLE

Judaism often refers to the destruction of the Holy Temple in Israel. Way back when, there was just one place of worship: the Holy Temple. Built over seven years by King Solomon, the Temple was ancient Israel's center of religion and culture. It served as the Jews' central place of worship for almost four hundred years, until it was destroyed by the Babylonians in 586 B.C.E.

A Second Temple was built in 516 B.C.E. The Romans destroyed it in C.E. 70. The only part of it that is left is the Western Wall, which is the Jews' holiest site in Jerusalem. The Temple is not to be rebuilt until the Messianic Age.

Steve used to go to High Holidays services with his Jewish wife. He could never figure out how to wear tallis correctly and was convinced that all the old men *davening* (rocking back and forth, mumbling or chanting) were really muttering to each other, "Look at that goy! Look at that goy!"

of the tallis are called *tzitziot*. They start with tight knots and end in a long loose fringe. The knots represent the negative commandments (think "thou shalt not"). The free fringe represents the positive commandments. Tzitziot remind the wearer of the whole Torah. They also tell us that a person can only be free if his lower nature is bound. (The word *religion* actually means "to bind back" in Hebrew and as a concept is not unique to Judaism.)

Amy Purcell of San Francisco remembers her first experience at temple with her Jewish boyfriend: "I asked my Jewish friend what to expect and she told me to just follow everyone else's lead. I was worried about when to sit, stand, kneel, and respond. She said, 'Don't worry. It's easy.' I found the service (which I continued to call a mass) beautiful and much more captivating than a Catholic mass. I was enthralled by the rabbi and what he said, and felt more spiritual than I had in a long time. At one point, we're all standing. The congregation was silent as the rabbi opened up the beautiful silver doors to retrieve the Torah. He pulled out the most stunning scroll. It was covered with cobalt-colored velvet and silver, which caught the light. I was awed and whispered to myself more loudly than I expected: 'Jesus Christ.'"

NO NEED FOR THE HEIMLICH MANEUVER

When you hear Yiddish and Hebrew, it often sounds like the speaker is trying to dislodge something from their throat. Words that are transliterated with a "ch" are the culprits . . . "chutzpah, challah. . . ."

WHAT'S THAT YOU SAY?

Don't get hung up on the language stuff too much. A lot of what you hear sprinkled into everyday speech is Yiddish, a High German language with a mixture of vocabulary from Hebrew and Slavic languages. Most Yiddish speakers are over the age of seventy, although the language is enjoying a minor renaissance among younger people. The Yiddish language is almost exclusive to Jews in and from Eastern and Central Europe.

You also might hear Hebrew, the official language of Israel. More important, most Jewish texts and prayers are written in Hebrew. Some texts and prayers are written in Aramaic. Most people would never know this, however, because the majority read the transliteration to follow along with the service. Some people do read

Hebrew, but few Jews in America speak it fluently enough to understand it. If you ever go to temple, there is no reason for anyone to ever know that you don't know Hebrew. Fake it. That's what transliteration is for. No one will know the difference. And you can take comfort in knowing that, half the time, most of the congregation is faking it, too.

THE JEWISH CALENDAR

You might have noticed that the Jewish calendar is not the same as the one we commonly use, the Gregorian calendar, and that's why the Jewish holidays seem to fall at different times each year. The Jewish calendar is a lunar calendar with 354 days per year. While the Gregorian is a solar calendar and runs on a 4-year cycle, the Jewish calendar has a 19-year cycle. In a Jewish leap year, a whole month is added rather than one day.

Obviously, the Jewish calendar is not based on Christ's birth. The Jewish calendar counts years since the creation of the Earth. According to Judaism, the Earth was created almost six thousand years ago. In fact, this book will be printed in the year 5760. Jews don't follow that B.C. and A.D. business either. Instead, all Jewish writing uses B.C.E. (Before the Common Era) and C.E. (Common Era).

A DEPRESSING HISTORY LESSON

Pogrom (pronounced "poh-grome") is Russian for "riot" or "devastation." Since the late nineteenth century it has referred to all violent anti-Jewish acts. In many instances, the Russian government instigated these outbreaks. While the term *pogrom* was applied a couple of hundred years ago, the Jews have been attacked by groups throughout history. The security and level of social acceptance that Jews in America experience today is rare in the long history of the Jewish religion. Jews have always been a nomadic people simply because they haven't been allowed to stay in one place for more than a few hundred years. The list on the next page might give insight as to why a certain paranoia, coupled with a fighter's instinct, has been passed down through the centuries of Jewish bloodlines.

HEBREW VERSUS YIDDISH TODAY

"On a bus in Tel Aviv, a mother was talking to her son in Yiddish and the son kept answering in Hebrew. After each of her son's responses, the mother would say, "No! Talk Yiddish! Talk Yiddish!"

An impatient Israeli overhears this and says, "Hey, lady, why do insist that he speaks Yiddish?"

The mother says, "I don't want him to forget he's a Jew."

IF YOU LEARN ONLY ONE HEBREW WORD . . .

Shalom (pronounced "sha-lome") means "hello," "good-bye," and "peace."

*"The pursuit of knowledge
for its own sake, an
almost fanatical love of
justice, and the desire for
personal independence —
these are the features of
the Jewish tradition which
make me thank my stars
that I belong to it."*

—ALBERT EINSTEIN

586 B.C.E.: Babylonians destroy the First Holy Temple and kill 1 million Jews.

C.E. 70: Roman emperor Vespasian's army captures Jerusalem, destroying the Second Holy Temple and killing 3 million Jews.

1096: First attacks on Jews in the First Crusade in Metz, France. Other mass expulsions happen in 1182, 1322, and 1420.

Eleventh and Twelfth Centuries: Crusades in Spain against the Jews and Muslims.

1290: Jews are expelled from England.

1388: Jews first get the boot from Germany, repeated in 1416, 1439, 1614, 1648, and the Nazi era.

1492: On the ninth of Av (a Jewish month), 150,000 Spanish Jews are forced onto crowded ships, beginning the expulsion of Jews from Spain. Portugal and Lithuania follow.

1521: Italy shows Jews the door, does it again in 1550, 1558, 1593, and 1597.

1648: Poland is invaded by the Russians from the east and the Swedes from the north. Some Poles turn on the Jews in their midst and conduct large-scale massacres. Hundreds of thousands of Jews are murdered. More than seven hundred communities are wiped out.

1880: Russian government decrees that a third of the Jews have to convert to Christianity, another third have to leave the country, and the remaining are to be murdered. The government-inspired pogroms led criminals and illiterate peasants to kill, rape, and steal from the Jews. Thousands of Jews die in massacres. Many emigrate.

1881: The Russian government-sponsored pogroms in Kiev, Warsaw, and the Ukraine.

1891: All Moscow Jews, some 20,000 people, are arrested, chained, and expelled.

1921: More Russian pogroms.

November 9, 1938: Kristallnacht, which means the night of broken glass in German—organized attacks by the Nazis on thousands of synagogues and Jewish shops in Germany and Austria. It was just the beginning.

1938: Mussolini's Racial Laws: no intermarriage, Jews are barred from state schools, no Aryan domestic servants in Jewish homes, no Jewish phone listings, no Jews in armed forces—and that's only some of it.

Why are Jews always on the receiving end? Because Jews don't believe in aggression. As it says in the Talmud: "Let a man always strive to be one of the persecuted rather than one of the persecutors."* This does not mean that Jews are taught to back down. They should try to survive; however, they should not become persecutors themselves.

THE HOLOCAUST

Hitler and the Nazi Party killed 6 million Jews in Europe in the 1930s and 1940s. In the worst Jewish massacre in modern times, more than one third of the world's Jewish population was wiped out. Even in such horrific circumstances, Jews called upon humor to stay sane: When the Nazis came to power, there were two types of Jews living in Germany—the optimists and the pessimists. The pessimists went into exile and the optimists went to the gas chambers.

The sadder truth is that even if the Jews could get out, the rest of the world offered very little help. In 1936, Chaim Weizmann, who later became the first president of Israel, accurately stated, "[For the Jews] the world is divided into places where they cannot live, and places which they cannot enter."

ISRAEL, THE PROMISED LAND

The basics of Judaism cannot be covered without talking about Israel. Israel has always played a prominent role in Jewish life. God promised the land of Israel to the Jewish people in the Book of Genesis. Throughout almost two thousand years of exile (C.E. 70–1948), wherever Jews have lived, they have prayed for the restora-

---

*Babylonian Talmud, *Baba Kamma* 93a

"The Jews constitute but one percent of the human race. . . . Properly the Jew ought hardly to be heard of, but he is heard of, has always been heard of. . . . He is as prominent on this planet as any other people. . . . He has made a marvelous fight in this world, in all the ages; and has done it all with his hands tied behind his back."

—MARK TWAIN*

*Excerpted from an article written in the summer of 1898, *The Man That Corrupted Hadleyburg and Other Stories and Essays*, Twain, Mark. New York, Harper & Brothers, 1900.

tion of their homeland. The State of Israel came into being in 1948 as a refuge for oppressed Jewry after World War II and the Holocaust. Despite this, it has always been a nation at war, as the land is coveted and threatened by neighboring Arab countries. Out of necessity, Israel built a very strong military. In fact, military service is mandatory for men and women once they reach the age of eighteen. Israel has become advanced in science and agriculture out of a similar need to survive.

Prior to the 1967 Six-Day War with Egypt, Jordan, and Syria, Israel was 8,000 square miles (about the size of New Jersey). After the Six Day War, it grew to 32,000 square miles. Most of the land has been returned as a result of various peace treaties. At the time of this writing, Israel was preparing to return the Golan Heights to Syria as part of a Middle East peace treaty.

Most important is the city of Jerusalem, an ancient holy link to the past for several world religions. During the exile, Jews were denied access to the old city. Since 1967, Jerusalem has been unified. The holiest part for Jews is the Western Wall, the only remaining structure of the Second Temple, also known as the Wailing Wall. It is a custom for people to write down a wish or a prayer onto slips of paper and insert it into crevices in the wall.

Every Jew can become a citizen of the tiny country just by saying that he or she desires to be one. Called the Law of Return, it is one of the earliest pieces of Israeli legislation. When a Jew immigrates to Israel, it is called "making *aliya*" (pronounced "ah-lee-ah"), which means ascent in Hebrew. (This is the same term for when someone is called to read from the Torah in temple.) Israelis often ask visiting Jews when they are going to make aliya. American Jews living in Israel may have dual citizenship. The same is true for Jews from England and a few other Western countries.

A Zionist is a supporter of the Jewish State of Israel. Not all Jews are Zionists. Likewise, many Zionists do not desire to live in Israel. They just feel better knowing that it's there.

Diaspora is a Greek word meaning "scattering." It is used to refer to the various communities of Jews living outside of Israel.

GIVE TILL IT HURTS

You might have noticed that Jews are exceptionally generous philanthropists. The Jewish ethical practice of giving money and other goods to those in need is called *tzedaka* (pronounced "tse-duh-kah") derived from the Hebrew root-word meaning "that which is right and just." Giving to the needy is not charity but an act of justice for society as a whole. Tzedaka attempts to rectify that which has gone wrong with society. Since ongoing reliance on charity is very demoralizing to the recipient, the highest form of tzedaka is to ensure that a person no longer needs charity in the long term. Anonymous charity is preferred.

Giving to the needy is not voluntary, it's mandatory. A Jew is not supposed to turn away from a person in need. It says in Deuteronomy 15:7: "If, however, there is a needy person among you . . . do not harden your heart and shut your hand against your needy kinsman. Rather, you must open your hand and lend him sufficient for whatever he needs." According to the Talmud, "Charity is equal in importance to all the other commandments combined."

THE JEWISH SOUL

We don't know exactly what it is, but Jews do believe there is a God-given spiritual thing inside each of us that makes us who we are. Call it the soul. Like a muscle, it can be fed and grown by following the commandments in the Torah—that is, by leading a good Jewish life. A San Francisco rabbi likens the soul to a stock portfolio that you can invest in and build up. We should only be so lucky that people pay as much attention to the well-being of their souls as that of their stock portfolios. As the soul is eternal, the investment is very long term. Word on the street is that there is tremendous pleasure for the soul in the world to come. Said pleasure is hard to describe, as most earthly pleasures are physical rather than spiritual.

IT'S A MITZVAH!

Mitzvah is the Hebrew word for commandment or religious duty. It is also loosely translated to mean a good deed. *Mitzvoth* (plural) tie into the Jewish focus on doing. While Jews constantly praise God, the religion is based more upon man's actions toward others than toward God. Doing mitzvoth, not merely talking about God, is what makes someone a good Jew. Mitzvoth range from giving to the poor to telling the truth, being honest in business, saying *broches* (blessings). Like a Jewish mother, it goes on and on.

While Judaism is old, it is not antiquated. The religion attempts to be applicable to the times. Most of the 613 mitzvoth set forth in the Torah are now defunct codes of temple, criminal, and agricultural law. Only about 100 are still relevant. Orthodox Jews follow a few dozen of them, which is more than most people.

"My friend Jack once told me that the difference between the attitudes of people of various religions on various activities (think things you might have done between Saturday night and Sunday morning in college) can be boiled down to "Catholics are ashamed, Jews are guilty, Protestants are just embarrassed.""

—Anonymous

Chapter 2

L'Chaim!: The Jewish Holidays

Maybe your Jewish friends eat ham and cheese sandwiches, don't keep the Sabbath, and can't speak Hebrew. This does not mean that they don't consider themselves to be Jewish. Out of the blue they will tell you that they have to fast for the next twenty-four hours because it's a Jewish holiday. You might think this behavior is crazy, but it is actually a common phenomenon. Everyone practices their religion in their own way, and Jews are no exception.

Basically, every Jewish holiday is just an excuse to get the loved ones together and eat. Even when fasting is a major component of the holiday, everyone gets to chow down after it's all said and done. If you can hold your own at a Jewish dinner table, you've won half the battle. If you're not particularly into food, you'd better learn to fake it. If you're on a diet, put it on hold.

Rivaling the Jews' love for food is their concern about appearances. Ladies, nothing too sexy. It's better to err on the side of conservatism. And you'll get extra points if your man looks presentable. That's about it. Don't worry about the dress code too much. So long as you don't look like a *shlepper*.

THE THREE-DAY JEW

This is someone who only practices Judaism three times a year: Rosh Hashanah, Yom Kippur, and Passover. Just as prevalent are the H2O Jews—Holidays: 2 Only—which are just Rosh Hashanah and Yom Kippur.

THE CHRISTMAS-EASTER JEWS

These are people who belong to a growing class of highly assimilated Jews who also celebrate some Christian holidays. They don't go to church or display nativity scenes, but they are known to open presents on December 25 and dye Easter eggs.

．．．．．．．．．．．．．．．．．．．．

"Anything worth saying is worth repeating a thousand times."

—JEWISH SAYING

It also helps to know how to make yourself heard in a crowd. Jews can make a lot of noise. Learn to project your voice. Don't fade into the woodwork. You may be perceived as aloof: "What? We're not good enough for her? She sits here all night hardly eating a thing, not saying one word." It's not the quality as much as the quantity that counts.

TIMING

Most holidays are really quick, two days or so. But there are a couple of marathon eight-day-ers. Jews living outside of Israel celebrate holidays for an extra day. This comes from way back, when there weren't accurate ways of determining exact dates. People observed holidays for an extra day to be sure they weren't violating a sacred day. To the Jew, it's better to overdo than risk falling short. We are nothing if not overachievers.

That's about it for the generalities. The specific holidays are divided into three sections here: Major Holidays You Must Know About, Holidays to Know About When Dating a Super-Jew, and Holidays Almost No One Celebrates But We Mention to Be Comprehensive.

Despite how we refer to them, the Jewish Holy Days are officially separated into Holidays, Festivals, and Fast Days. Fortunately, Yom Kippur is the only prescribed fast day in the Torah. Almost all the other fasts commemorate major calamities that have befallen the Jewish people. Enterprising individuals and communities can also start their own annual fasting days to commemorate personal or communal tragedies.

In a Jewish fast, there is no eating or drinking whatsoever. Most fast days are from sunrise to sunset. The exceptions are the two most popular fasts: Yom Kippur and Tisha B'av. They go from sunset to sunset. Jews like to play the martyr. They go for the long fast.

MAJOR HOLIDAYS YOU MUST KNOW ABOUT

High Holy Days

WHAT:	Rosh Hashanah and Yom Kippur
WHEN:	Early fall (September/October)
LASTS:	Rosh Hashanah and Yom Kippur, both last one or two days, depending on how observant one is. Starts and ends at sundown
WHERE:	Temple for services, dinner and breaking of the fast at home or with friends
WHY:	Ten Days of Penitence
AKA:	Jewish New Year (Rosh Hashanah), Day of Judgment (Yom Kippur), Days of Awe (both)
IMPORTANCE:	✡✡✡✡
FOOD:	Rosh Hashanah: Apples and honey (for a sweet New Year), round *challah* (instead of braided for a year of unbroken continuity), brisket, chicken soup, *tzimmes*, honey cake
PROPS:	*Shofar*
WHAT TO BRING:	Kosher wine, pound cake (marble if possible)
WHAT TO WEAR:	Conservative dress or suit; no leather (to avoid animal cruelty as well as a reminder of warfare)
WHAT TO SAY:	*"L'Shanah tova tikatevu,"* means "May you be inscribed for a good year," or just *"Shanah tova,"* meaning "Happy New Year." Saying "Happy New Year" in English will also do. Also *"Gut yontif"* means "Happy Holiday" in Yiddish.

Some may be disappointed to hear that the High Holy Days have nothing to do with marijuana. These same people will take comfort in learning that there is a big feast at the end. But you've got to suffer a little to get there.

The High Holy Days are comprised of two distinct holidays separated by Ten Days of Penitence. The first sounds like a sneeze— Rosh Hashanah (pronounced "rush ha-shah-nah"). It really means "head of the year" in Hebrew. The second is Yom Kippur (pronounced "yum kip-poor") which means "Day of Atonement."

HOLIDAYS, FESTIVALS, AND FASTING DAYS

Holidays:

Rosh Hashanah, Yom Kippur, Sukkoth, Passover, Shevuoth

Festivals:

Hanukkah, Purim, Yom Ha-Atzmaut, Tu B'Shvat

Fasting Days:

Yom Kippur, Fast of Esther, Fast of Gedaliah, Fast of the Tenth of Tevet, Fast of the Seventeenth of Tammuz, Fast of the Ninth of Av

• • • • • • • • • • • • • • • • •

Practicing Jews go to temple on Rosh Hashanah and Yom Kippur. In areas with large Jewish populations, Rosh Hashanah and Yom Kippur are practically legal holidays with most schools and businesses closed in observance. The synagogues get extremely crowded. Many are forced to divide the congregation in half and do services in shifts. Most require their congregations to buy or reserve tickets. Some even assign seats.

On that note, women shouldn't be shocked if they are relegated to the nosebleed section while their boyfriends get to sit on the main floor, and men shouldn't be surprised if they get stuck with a bunch of guys while their girlfriends sit upstairs and schmooz with the ladies. This Orthodox practice of separating the men and the women predates political correctness.

ROSH HASHANAH

The newcomer to Judaism might be chagrined to learn the Jewish New Year does not entail the revelry of the secular New Year's celebration. Fortunately, it's in the fall so there are no conflicts with December 31. Most Jews go to services on the first day of Rosh Hashanah, and many go the second day as well.

SHOFAR BLOWING

The high point of the Rosh Hashanah service is when the shofar, or ram's horn, is blown. In most temples, the same member of the congregation blows the shofar every year. It takes both remarkable lung capacity and a rare skill to evoke the desired sounds out of a sawed-off ram's horn. When done right, it is quite awe-inspiring.

Since biblical times, the shofar has been used to announce great events. It is supposed to convey the mood of the Israelites standing at the foot of Mount Sinai when God gave Moses the Torah and, of course, the Ten Commandments. It is still used in Israel to announce the coming of the Sabbath and a new president's inauguration.

CASTING OUT SINS

There is a special ceremony on Rosh Hashanah held on the water's edge called *Tashlich*, "the casting out of sins." People write their sins of the past year on pieces of paper and toss them into the water. By doing this they get to see all their sins literally washed away. At some temples, people toss pieces of bread into the water. The bread serves to symbolize sin and feeds local wildlife to boot.

TEN DAYS OF PENITENCE

This is the period between Rosh Hashanah and Yom Kippur when Jews repent for their sins of the past year and think about self-improvement for the coming year. It's said that on Rosh Hashanah the sound of the shofar reaches the ears of God and reminds Him to open the Book of Life. According to legend, in this book God writes everyone's destiny for the year to come. God decides who will be rich and who will be poor, who will rise up in the world and who will fall down, who will be peaceful and who will be miserable.

The Book of Life is broken into three sections: a section for the righteous, a section for the wicked, and one for those in between. The righteous are immediately inscribed for a good life for the next year. The wicked are condemned to death. The in-betweens have the Ten Days of Penitence to redeem themselves. No one knows in what section his name will be written, so it's best to repent.

SAY YOU'RE SORRY

Jews distinguish between sins committed against God and those committed against man. Offenses against God may be forgiven if the sinner confesses and promises not to repeat the sin. Offenses against man are only forgiven by God when the sinner makes amends to the person wronged.

Jewish tradition regards repentance as so important that one who truly repents is considered superior to one who has not sinned. However, atonement is a process. The concept of repentance is called *t'shuvah,* which means "returning" in Hebrew. An individual can be forgiven of his sins by turning back to God. A Jew can't sin all year, be forgiven on Yom Kippur, and go right back to sinning. He must truly change his evil ways. According to the Talmud, someone is truly penitent if the opportunity to commit the same sin presents itself twice and the person doesn't sin.

THINGS TO DO IN TEMPLE

1. Tie macramé knots in the prayer book ribbon. Untie knots. Repeat.
2. Pick out best- and worst-dressed people in the crowd. Whisper comments to neighbors.
3. Make up stories about random members of the congregation.
4. Flip through prayer books looking for especially bizarre passages.
5. Ponder own existence.

YOM KIPPUR

There once was a rabbi who was a compulsive golfer. It was such a problem that one Yom Kippur, he stole out of the house early in the morning to catch a quick nine holes by himself. An angel happened to notice and immediately alerted his superior that a grievous sin was being committed on Earth. On the sixth hole, God caused a mighty wind to take the ball directly from the tee to the cup for a miraculous and dramatic hole in one.

The angel was horrified. "Lord," he said, "you call this a punishment?"

"Sure," answered God with a smile. "Who can he tell?"

Joking aside, this Holy Day is pretty somber, as the name—Day of Atonement—suggests. Yom Kippur requires Jews to do things they would not do on any other day of the year. For an example, as a way of cleansing themselves of sin, Jews fast from sundown on the eve of Yom Kippur until sunset the next day. As a people obsessed with food, Jews tend to find this very difficult. In addition to starving themselves for a day, they also have to atone for their sins. This is also tough, since most Jews find it hard to stop arguing for five minutes, let alone admit they were actually wrong about something. Finally, much of the day is spent in temple, which can get pretty boring.

In the *Al Chet*, a prayer said on Yom Kippur, Jews ask for forgiveness for a multitude of sins: malicious gossip, sexual immorality, gluttony, narrow-mindedness, fraud, falsehood, hatred without cause, arrogance, insolence, irreverence, hypocrisy, passing judgment, exploitation, bribery, giving way to hostile impulses, and running to do evil. What's your favorite?

This forgiveness on Yom Kippur business goes way back. The official word is that on the same day that Moses came down from Sinai with the second set of tablets with the Ten Commandments, he told the Israelites that God was letting them off the hook for the whole idolatry/golden calf incident. *Whew!*

Part of the atonement process is afflicting one's soul. This traditionally calls for abstaining from:

Eating and drinking

Sex

Bathing (for pleasure; it's okay to bathe if you stink)

Anointing the body with oil (an ancient hygienic practice)

Wearing leather (shoes, belts, and handbags included)

Have fun!

Breaking the Fast (aka the Big Payoff)

The indisputably best part of the High Holy Days is the meal marking the end of the Yom Kippur fast, called Break the Fast. All finally feels right with the world at this celebration, as Jews are reunited with food. The fare is meant to be light so as not to upset the stomach after a day of fasting. Despite this, dieters beware: Some families use Break the Fast as an excuse to put on an all-out feast, with rooms full of food and dozens of guests noshing. To some it is worth it to fast and go to temple just to be able to go to a Break the Fast afterward.

High Holy Days Tip Sheet

1. Those who are curious about High Holiday services (but not enough to go to temple) can find virtual services on several Internet sites such as Virtual Jerusalem and Maven.

2. If you are going to temple, wear nice shoes but make sure they are comfortable; there is a lot of standing during services. Also, parking lots fill up fast, so you might have to walk a long way from the car.

3. If you are going to temple, try to arrive a little early to get one of the comfortable seats. Otherwise you are likely to end up on a folding chair put out for the overflow.

4. Encourage your partner to start eating less and less at meals a few days before Yom Kippur. This is said to shrink the stomach and make fasting easier.

5. Let your significant other sleep as late as possible on Yom Kippur—fewer hours of fasting, fewer hours of crabbiness.

6. Avoid kissing, dancing cheek to cheek, or whispering sweet nothings on Yom Kippur. From not eating, your partner's breath is

WHO DOESN'T FAST

While fasting is a major part of Yom Kippur, health is also extremely important. Pregnant women, nursing mothers, people who are ill, elderly, or those who must take medication do not fast. Kids under nine are not supposed to fast either. Fasting is supposed to be slowly introduced so that children can fast by age twelve for girls or thirteen for boys. Why is it that women always have to start watching what they eat at a younger age?

YOM KIPPUR WAR

On the highest of holy days in October 1973, Egypt and Syria launched a surprise attack on Israel. The effort was to regain Arab territory won by Israel in the 1967 Six-Day War. Israel defeated its enemies in less than three weeks.

THINGS YOU'LL OVERHEAR AT A BREAK THE FAST

"Where's the *kugel*?"

"How long did you fast?"

"I only drank water."

"You can tell who didn't fast. They are being much more civil."

. . . .

likely to be strong enough to strip paint off walls. This is exacerbated by not being able to drink water, chew gum, or brush teeth.

7. Do not bring wine or alcohol to a Break the Fast unless you want a lot of drunk Jews on your hands.

═══════════════════════════════

PASSOVER

WHAT:	Celebrates the Exodus from Egypt
WHEN:	March or April, around Easter
LASTS:	Eight days
WHERE:	Home
WHY:	To remind Jews that they were once slaves; to celebrate the Exodus from Egypt and freedom for Jews everywhere.
AKA:	Pesach, Pesah
IMPORTANCE:	✡✡✡✡
FOOD:	Jews do not eat anything made with yeast (and a whole slew of other stuff) for eight days.
PROPS:	Seder plate, *Haggadah*, matzah
WHAT TO BRING:	Flowers are safest. If you must bring food, go to a Jewish bakery and see what they have for Passover or anything in the grocery store that says "Kosher for Pesach" on the box. Or, bring a bottle of kosher wine.

WAY BACK IN EGYPT-LAND

If you haven't seen Charlton Heston in *The Ten Commandments*, rent it. It's quite impressive. You know the story: After ten plagues, the Egyptian pharaoh finally lets the children of Israel out of bondage. Moses parts the Red Sea, and they spend forty years wandering in the desert.

TODAY

During the eight days of Passover, Jews eat matzah, which is an unleavened crackerlike bread. This is the same stuff the Israelites ate when they were fleeing from the Egyptians and couldn't wait for the bread to rise. When made badly, matzah tastes like cardboard. When made well, it still tastes like cardboard. The best thing that can be said about it is that leftover matzah can be used by dieters in place of rice cakes. In preparation for Passover, Conservative and Orthodox Jews must clean the kitchen from top to bottom and throw out all bread products and *hametz*, leavened food that cannot be eaten during Passover. The term *hametz* also refers to dishes and utensils that observant Jews put away during Passover. There are special dishes that are reserved for use during the holiday for those who really get into cleaning their kitchen.

But Passover is more than just the Exodus from Egypt and the eating of matzah. As with other Jewish holidays, this one uses rituals to recount the Jews' suffering. Seder means "order" in Hebrew, a word that well explains the very specific sequence of the ceremony. The Haggadah, which is the Hebrew word for "story," serves as a how-to book, a study guide and a songbook for the seder. It is read every year during the first two Passover dinners. This can take anywhere from fifteen minutes to four hours, depending on the people involved—and how hungry they are.

As a non-Jew, you will be a seder target. Most seders have at least one non-Jewish guest. They actually seem to be interested in the seder. The official reason for inviting non-Jews is to remember how we were strangers in the land of Egypt.

SEDER SPECIFICS

The Seder Plate

The most prominent item on the table is the seder plate. It is usually large and decorated with Passover symbols. These plates can run the gamut from family heirlooms to kindergarten art projects. The seder plate includes a variety of symbolic, albeit unappetizing, foods:

✿ The shank bone represents the animal sacrifice the Israelites made in ancient times.

✿ *Karpas* is any green vegetable to represent spring and the renewal of life. It also another reminder of the poor diet the slaves

BUSTED!

"*I was going out with a non-Jew,*" said Pete Richter of San Francisco. "*It was approaching Passover and she inquired about the history behind the holiday. Little did she know that my understanding of the history of Passover was acquired from the movie* The Ten Commandments, *which I had seen about a zillion times. My girlfriend already thought I watched too much TV, so as I started telling her the story I didn't tell her where my knowledge came from. She was very impressed as I went into great detail about the story of Moses and the Pharaoh. Just when I was winding up my story, I said, 'So then, Yul Brynner conceded that he could not beat Moses.' Upon which she interrupted and said, 'Wait a minute! Yul Brynner! How did Yul Brynner get into this story?' At this point I was busted and found out for a fraud, further convincing her that I do indeed watch too much TV.*"

THE PARTING OF THE RED SEA, DEMYSTIFIED!

In biblical times, the Red Sea was actually called the Sea of Reeds, which may scientifically explain Moses' miraculous parting. The Jews were able to walk across the reeds at low tide while the chariot wheels got caught and the Egyptians drowned.

· ·

had in Egypt. It is dipped into salt water to represent the bitter tears of slavery. Parsley is almost always the karpas of choice. Take a nibble to get rid of that pesky *gefilte* fish breath.

✡ The roasted or hard-boiled egg (still in shell), the *beitzah*, represents Israel. Like eggs that become harder as they cook, Jews say that they toughen their resolve during times of trouble. It is also a symbol of fertility. Finally, it is a sign of mourning and therefore a reminder of the destruction of the Holy Temples.

✡ *Maror*, bitter herbs, usually a piece of horseradish, symbolize the bitterness of slavery. Seder participants are also supposed to think of the bitterness of the life of those living in communities that are not allowed to practice Judaism.

✡ *Charoset*, a mixture of apples, nuts, wine, and cinnamon, represents the mortar the slaves used to make bricks for the Egyptian pyramids. This actually tastes pretty good and is spread between matzah for a sandwich.

The Four Cups of Wine

Drinking wine is a mitzvah (good deed). Jews drink a small amount of wine at every Jewish celebration. It is a symbol of Jewish freedom, victories, joyous moments of the past, and dreams for the future. During the seder, participants get to drink four ceremonial cups of wine.

The Four Questions

These questions relay the importance of the seder in a way that even a child can understand. It's very cute to hear a child sing the Four Questions. It's somewhat pathetic to hear them coming from an adult. If there are no children in the house, borrowing a small child to sing the Four Questions is recommended.

For those of you with inquiring minds, the Four Questions are:

1. Why do we eat only matzah and no bread on this night?
2. Why do we eat bitter herbs on this night?
3. Why do we dip our food in salt water two times on this night?
4. Why do we recline when we eat on this night?

The Afikoman

There is always a plate on the seder table with three matzahs wrapped in a special cover or linen. The middle matzah, the *afikoman*, mysteriously disappears from the stack during the first part of the seder. Later, the children tear up the house in search of it. When it is found, the afikoman is sold back to the leader of the seder for a small price. This not only allows the seder to be completed but teaches Jewish children important bargaining skills early in life.

A True Story

Alison Weiss (née Johnson) still laughs when she recalls her first Passover at her in-laws. "I was helping my little nephews, who attend a very religious day school, set the Passover table. They'd made matzah covers, a matzah plate, a seder plate, and so on. They'd also made a little baby figurine in a basket.

"In a very loud voice, I picked up the figurine and said, 'Who's this? Baby Jesus?' All surrounding conversations came to a halt. My two-year-old nephew yelled, 'No! It's Baby Moses!'

"It took me a couple of years to live that down!"

Another True Story

One year, Mike Beerman observed Passover by eating nothing but bean burritos from Taco Bell. As tortillas contain leavening agents, some took issue with this. Mike, however, stood firmly in his conviction that he was properly paying tribute to the Jews' exodus from Egypt. "If I had to get the hell out of Dodge," said Mike, "I'd stop by Taco Bell. The bean burrito is cheap, fast, and filling. It's the perfect food for a people on the run."

Yet Another True Story

"I dated a nice Jewish boy for a while in college in Ohio. During my junior year, his family came in from Los Angeles to gather what was apparently every Jew within a ten-mile radius and have a seder. I was feeling a bit uncomfortable, largely due to the fact that I didn't understand a word of what anyone was saying. I turned to the Asian guy sitting next to me and quite loudly said, 'Hey! Looks like we're the only non-Jews in here! I have

GEFILTE FISH

In Yiddish, gefilte means "stuffed." This was a staple for Eastern European Jews who couldn't afford to buy a whole fish. Instead, they would grind up pieces of leftover fish and pack it all together. Garnish (sparingly) with horseradish.

"NEXT YEAR IN JERUSALEM!"

At the end of each Passover seder, participants toast "Next year in Jerusalem!" This is not optimism about extra vacation time but hope that in the following year all Jews will be free and living in the Promised Land.

Next year in Jerusalem. The year after, how about a nice cruise?

. . . .

no idea what's going on!' Unfortunately, instead of the camaraderie I was looking for, he turned and told me that he was Jewish, too."—Shelley Weaver

One More True Story

"My dad is Jewish, Mom was a converted Catholic from her first marriage, and I was primarily raised by my Protestant maternal grandparents. Needless to say, I had little focused religious upbringing much less a real understanding of Judaism. But I always loved being 'Jewish' and gravitated toward Jewish friends and boyfriends, all of whom were not that religious either. However, one of my boyfriends was a serious Jew. One day while we were going out, I found myself at a Jewish bakery in Berkeley. I was thrilled to find that all of their delicious loaves of bread were half off. So I bought three loaves planning to surprise him with not only this great bread, but 'Oy, what a bargain!' You can imagine the tender look of surprise and embarrassment when I presented the loaves to his family on Passover."

—Kristy Beldner

FAVORITE PASSOVER RECIPES

If you really want to wow them, bring one of these tasty dishes to the next seder you attend.

ALMOND MACAROONS
Yield 40

> *¹/₂ teaspoon almond extract*
> *4 egg whites, at room temperature, beaten stiff but not dry*
> *¹/₂ pound finely ground blanched almonds*
> *¹/₂ cup sugar*
> *toasted slivered almonds for garnish*

Add almond extract to beaten whites. Mix almonds with sugar and slowly fold into whites. Pipe or spoon onto oiled wax paper–lined baking sheets. Top with slivered almonds. Bake at 300 degrees for 30–40 minutes or until lightly browned.

PECAN BRITTLE

Yield 2 dozen

> *3 egg whites*
> *1 cup brown sugar*
> *1 cup chopped pecans*
> *24 pecan halves*

Beat whites and slowly add the sugar. Mixture should be very stiff. Fold in chopped nuts by hand. Drop by spoonfuls onto greased, lined cookie sheets. Press flat and top with pecan half. Bake at 275 degrees for 30 minutes or until shiny but firm.

PASSOVER BAGELS

Yield 10–12

> *$^1/_2$ cup cold water*
> *pinch of salt*
> *$^1/_2$ cup vegetable oil*
> *1 tablespoon sugar*
> *1 cup matzah meal*
> *3 large eggs*
> *Seeds or onions to sprinkle on top (optional)*

Combine water, salt, oil, and sugar in a pan and bring to a boil. Beat in the matzah meal. Cool. Add eggs one at a time, beating well. Drop in heaping tablespoons onto greased pan. Make hole in center. Bake at 350 degrees for 30 minutes or until golden. Sprinkle seeds or onions on top.

TIP

Godiva chocolates are not a good hostess gift for Passover. Regardless of how elegant they are, they are not kosher for Passover.

MATZAH AND CHEESE KUGEL

Serves 6 as a main dish, 10 as a side dish

> *5 eggs*
> *1 cup milk*
> *1 pound cottage cheese*
> *¹/₄ cup honey*
> *salt*
> *¹/₂ teaspoon ground cinnamon*
> *4 matzahs, broken*
> *¹/₂ cup slivered almonds*

Preheat oven to 350 degrees. Grease a 2-quart baking dish. Beat eggs with milk. Add cottage cheese, honey, salt, and cinnamon. Place half of the matzah pieces in the baking dish. Pour half of the mixture on top and sprinkle with almonds. Cover with remaining matzah pieces and then the cheese mixture. Bake 40 minutes or until slightly browned and crunchy on top.

HANUKKAH

WHAT:	The Festival of Lights
WHEN:	December, conveniently close to Christmas
LASTS:	Eight nights
WHERE:	Homes of friends and family
WHY:	To celebrate the victory of the Maccabees (Jewish patriots) over the Assyrians and the Jews' freedom once again
AKA	Chanukkah, Hannukah—there are spelling variations because some Hebrew letters don't translate directly.
IMPORTANCE:	✡✡
FOOD:	*Latkes* (potato pancakes, prounounced "lot-keys")
PROPS:	*Dreidel*, Hanukkah gelt (money or chocolate)
WHAT TO BRING:	Small presents, *gelt*
WHAT TO WEAR:	Casual dress

SING ALONG

Dreidel, dreidel, dreidel
I made it out of clay.
And when it's dry and ready
Oh, dreidel I shall play.

This is one of the stories that inspired this book for all of you unsuspecting non-Jews. A nice but crafty Jewish guy thought he'd pulled one over on his new non-Jewish girlfriend. He convinced her that all Jews receive eight presents, one for each night, during Hanukkah (pronounced "ha-new-kah"). And not little tokens of affection either—full-fledged gifts like stereo equipment, expensive dinners, and nice clothes. Never having dated a Jewish guy before, the girl-friend believed him. By Day 6 the girl was almost broke.

Finally her friends filled her in: Hanukkah presents are primarily given to children and usually consist of Hanukkah gelt, small toys, small sums of money, and so on. Gifts are rarely given all eight days, especially not to grown-ups. The holiday is usually celebrated with a low-key Hanukkah party and by lighting the menorah, adding one candle each night.

Why Hanukkah Is Called the Festival of Lights

Believe it or not, this is the only Jewish holiday that honors a war victory. In 168 B.C.E., the Seleucid king of Syria Antiochus Epiphanes tried to force the Greek religion on the Jews. He made it a crime to teach the Torah and perform Jewish rituals such as circumcision. His armies installed idols in the Temple and priests sacrificed pigs to the Greek gods. An old man named Mattathias refused to allow this in his town and killed the man who tried to slaughter swine in the town's place of worship. He and his five sons then fled to the hills and organized the rebellion that saved Judea (ancient Israel). In 165 B.C.E., after a narrow victory, the soldiers, led by Judah the Maccabee, Mattathias's warrior son, reclaimed the Holy Temple.

The next part of the story is what most Jews remember. Once back inside the Temple, the soldiers could only find what appeared to be enough oil to light the lamps for one day. The rededication and purification process, however, takes eight days. Miraculously, the oil burned for exactly eight days. Hanukkah means "dedication" in Hebrew.

The rabbis who codified Jewish law in the Talmud felt that it was better to focus on the oil and the freedom to light the menorah in the Temple than on the military victory. The goal of the Jews is really to be free, not to triumph. Thus, most of the holiday talk is of the menorah and the oil rather than of the battle.

LATKES

These potato pancakes can be eaten with applesauce or sour cream but never maple syrup. They are delicious but very greasy. It is rumored that in the time of the Maccabees, they lit a latke by mistake and it burned for eight days. Okay, maybe not, but the post-latke heartburn usually lasts just as long.

SHAMMES

The ninth candle on the menorah that is used to light the other candles.

. . . .

Today, in celebration, American and European Jews fry potato pancakes, or latkes, in vats of oil. With a similar disregard for their cholesterol intake, Israelis eat jelly doughnuts, or *sufganiyot* (pronounced suf-gan-ee-yote). Both greasy delights symbolize the Maccabees' victory and miracle oil.

Jews commemorate the event by lighting a nine-pronged candelabra, called a *menorah*. On the first day, they light one candle, then add one on each consecutive day. As they say the blessings, they light the candles with the flame of the *shammes*. Like the Shabbat candles, the Hanukkah candles must burn until they go out by themselves. No one blows them out. Hanukkah candles cannot be used for any purpose other than celebrating the miracle. For example, don't use the light to see or read by.

Jews traditionally place the menorah in the window both to celebrate Hanukkah and as a symbol of pride in being Jewish. The rabbis say to put a menorah in the window to advertise the miracle and to spread the light to others. However, some paranoid Jews have been known to place the menorah in the kitchen sink to prevent the house from burning down, God forbid.

===

BLESSINGS OVER THE CANDLES

ON THE FIRST NIGHT ONLY, SAY THE SHEHECHEYANU:

Ba-ruch atah Adonai elohe-nu melech ha-olom sheh-heche-ah-nu ve-ki-yi-mo-nu ve-higi-a-nu laz-man ha-zeh.

Blessed art thou, O Lord our God, King of the universe, who has granted us life, sustained us and enabled us to reach this occasion.

ON ALL NIGHTS:

Bar-uch atah Adonai elohe-nu melech ha-olom asher ki-di-shanu be-mitz-votav vit-zi-va-nu le-had-lik ner shel ha-nu-kah.

Blessed art thou, O Lord our God, King of the universe, who has sanctified us with His commandments and commanded us to kindle the Hanukkah light.

Ba-ruch atah Adonai elohe-nu melech ha-olom she-a-ta ni-sim la-vo-tei-nu ba-ya-mim ha-hem baz'man ha-zeh.

Blessed art thou, O Lord our God, King of the universe, who performed miracles for our forefathers.

A True Story

Suzie and Todd are married. Todd is Jewish. When asked if they had any funny stories about the early years of their marriage, Todd said, "Yeah, our first Hanukkah, Suzie blew out the candles!" He was so mad that he refused to light the candles for the rest of Hanukkah that year.

TO GIVE OR NOT TO GIVE

Not only are Hanukkah gifts small, but the giving is not widespread. Jews don't give gifts to all their friends and colleagues for Hanukkah like people do at Christmas. The custom of giving small gifts is believed to have started in seventeenth-century Poland, where parents gave children money to give to their teachers. Eventually, parents gave the children small coins as well, as a reward for performing their tasks and for studying. By the eighteenth century, the custom expanded as poor yeshiva students started going to the houses of rich Jews to receive Hanukkah gelt. As Jews had more contact with Christians, they were influenced by the custom of giving presents for Christmas and began giving gifts in addition to money for Hanukkah.

A TYPICAL HANUKKAH HAUL

When Jenny Zimmerman was a child, she usually got presents on all eight nights, but the gift-giving spirit died a slow death around Night 5 as her parents ran out of ideas.

Night 1: A gift she really wanted
Night 2: A gift she thought was okay
Night 3: Something her mom wanted her to have, like a book
Night 4: Stationery
Night 5: Underwear

GELT

Yiddish for money. Also, chocolates wrapped in gold foil to resemble coins.

TOP TEN REASONS TO LIKE HANUKKAH

10. No roof damage from reindeer

9. Never a silent night when you're among your Jewish loved ones

8. If someone screws up on their gift, there are seven more days to make up for it

7. Betting Hanukkah gelt on candle races

6. You can use your fireplace

5. Naked spin-the-dreidel games

4. Fun waxy buildup on the menorah

3. No awkward explanations of virgin birth

2. Cheer optional

1. No Irving Berlin songs

. . . .

Night 6: One of those pens that wrote in fifteen colors

Night 7: Socks

Night 8: Something so meager that Jenny was happy that Hanukkah was finally over

LET MY LATKES BIND!

Feeling nostalgic for the Hanukkah parties of her youth, Liz Diamond decided to throw a grown-up version. Being the hostess, Liz undertook the serious task of making the latkes herself. She molded the potato mix into pancakes as her guests watched in awe. The pan sputtered with oil as she continued to press the potato mixture. The mixture wouldn't stay molded. She pressed again. Alas, the latkes wouldn't bind!

Liz fretted and called her mother. The solution was more egg. When that didn't work, cell phones were whipped out as the guests made the requisite call to the family cook. "More baking powder!" "More flour!"

Finally, with oil coating the flour and slicking guests' hair, the latkes bound and they feasted. And it was good.

Here's a recipe to have on hand in case you ever end up at a party like Liz's. Bubbe had to grate her potatoes by hand. So, thank your lucky stars that we have food processors today. If you're really lazy, frozen hash browns will do.

LATKES

Makes 15 potato pancakes

4 large potatoes (peeled)
1 large onion
1 egg
1 teaspoon salt
¼ teaspoon pepper
2 tablespoons flour
½ teaspoon baking powder
½ cup vegetable shortening or oil
Astringent for postfrying facial clean-up (optional)

Grate potatoes and onion using a grater with large holes. Transfer to colander. Squeeze mixture to press out as much liquid as possible. Add egg, salt, pepper, flour, and baking powder. Mix well. Heat shortening or oil in deep, heavy 10–12 inch frying pan. For each pancake, drop about 2 tablespoons of the mixture into the pan and flatten with a spoon so that each cake is $2^1/_2$–3 inches in diameter. Fry over medium heat on each side until golden brown and crisp. Add more shortening or oil when necessary. Total frying time: 4–5 minutes. Place cooked pancakes on paper towels to sop up grease. Serve hot with applesauce or sour cream on the side.

Tip

A gift exchange or grab bag is a common element at Hanukkah parties. Each guest is asked to bring an inexpensive wrapped gift. Be sure that whatever you bring is not even slightly related to Christmas. Non-Jews have inadvertently erred in bringing things like festive lights and even Christmas CDs as grab-bag gifts. This is not the way to blend in.

SHORT SUMMARY OF EVERY JEWISH HOLIDAY

They tried to kill us.

We won.

Let's eat!

. . . .

DREIDEL

Dreidel (pronounced "dray-dull") is the Yiddish word for top. In Hebrew it's called a *sevivon,* or a spinning top.

Carved or painted on each side of the dreidel are the Hebrew letters nun, gimmel, heh, and peh. They stand for the Hebrew words nes gadol haya poh, "A great miracle happened here." Outside of Israel, the letter peh is replaced by a shin, standing for sham, or "there."

The game dreidel is a bit like gambling, so ante up. Here are the rules:

1. Every player receives the same number of coins, nuts, or similar items with which to bet.

2. Before spinning the dreidel, each player puts the same amount into a *kupah,* or kitty.

3. The first player spins the dreidel. According to the letter it falls on, do the following:

   Nun = no win/no lose (do nothing)   Heh = take half the kitty

   Gimmel = take the kitty   Shin = lose what you bet

4. The next player spins. Any player who loses all his or her funds is out of the game. The game continues until one player has all of the funds.

LAWS OF SABBATH

Most people see the Shabbat laws as:

✡ No working

✡ No driving

✡ No using electricity

The Laws of the Sabbath listed below are the official line of Judaism:

✡ Peace within ourselves

✡ Peace between people

✡ Peace between people and nature

✡ Peace between people and God

SHABBAT

WHAT:	The day of rest
WHEN:	Every Friday starting at sundown
LASTS:	One day, starts and ends at sundown
WHERE:	Temple or home
WHY:	After creating the universe, God rested
AKA:	The Sabbath, Shabbes (Yiddish)
IMPORTANCE:	✡✡✡✡✡ *(most important holiday)*
FOOD:	Challah
PROPS:	2 Shabbat candles, candlesticks, and *kiddush* cup
WHAT TO BRING:	Kosher wine, dessert, flowers
WHAT TO SAY:	*Shabbat Shalom* (pronounced "shah-baht shah-lome"), meaning "peaceful Sabbath," or "Good Shabbes" ("shah-biss"), meaning "good Sabbath."

Where life is in danger, Sabbath laws do not apply.

—JEWISH PROVERB

The Sabbath is supposed to be a pretty big deal. The purpose is to make the sixth day of the week holy and create a taste of the Messianic Age one day each week. It is not intended to be a day of rest. Rest is a by-product. Instead, it is a time to be devoted to family, Torah study, and worship. For over 5,500 years of Jewish history, it was. But that was in the Old Country. Few Jews in America keep the Sabbath as originally outlined. That doesn't stop people from telling a lot of Jewish jokes about not obeying the laws of the Sabbath, or keeping them:

> There once was a businessman who warned his son against marrying a non-Jew—a shiksa. The son protested, "But she's converting to Judaism."
> "It doesn't matter," the old man said. "A shiksa will cause problems."
> One day after the wedding, the father asked his son why he wasn't at the family store.
> "It's Shabbat," the son said.

The father was surprised. "But we always work on Saturday. It's our busiest day."

"I won't work anymore on Saturday," the son insisted, "because my wife wants us to go to synagogue on Shabbat."

"See," the father said, "I told you marrying a shiksa would cause problems."

While few strictly observe the Sabbath, people will have special Friday night Shabbat dinners on occasion. Inviting non-Jewish guests over for Shabbat dinners is part of the tradition. These dinners differ from the rest of the week in a couple of small ways. First, they tend to be a little fancier—tablecloths are involved. Second, people say a few short prayers at the beginning of the meal.

BLESSING THE CHILDREN

At the beginning of the Sabbath, the father traditionally gives these blessings to his children in the hope that they become great Jews and great people. The blessing for sons is: "May God make you like Ephraim and Menashe" (Joseph's two sons). To daughters: "May God make you like Sarah, Rebecca, Rachel, and Leah" (Judaism's matriarchs).

LIGHTING THE CANDLES

Before the meal is served, the woman of the house lights the Shabbat candles. Traditionally, she covers her head with a scarf or shawl. Then she lights the candles and shields her eyes with her hands as she says the prayer. *Tip:* Do not blow out the Shabbat candles. They are supposed to burn all the way down.

BLESSINGS OVER FOOD AND WINE

These blessings are called the *kiddush* and the *hamotzi* (pronounced "hah-mot-zee"). Religious Jews say them before each meal, while others just say them at holidays.

The kiddush is:
Ba-ruch atah Adonai elohe-nu melech ha-olam bo-rei pri ha-gufen.

SHABBES GOY

Shabbes goy is the Yiddish term for a non-Jew hired to cook and do household chores on the Sabbath. In Europe, up until the turn of the century, Jews lived in segregated communities known as shtetls (pronounced "shteh-tuls"). *Shabbes goys* and law enforcement officials were often their only contact with non-Jews.

SAY NO TO SICKLY SWEET WINE

Kosher wine doesn't have to taste bad. One hint: stay away from Concord grape. The following wines don't taste like cough syrup:

✡ Hagafen Cellars

✡ Kedem Royal Wine Co.'s Baron Herzog, Weinstock, Gamla, and Yarden labels

✡ Carmel Valley

✡ Shapiro's Winery

✡ Mount Maroma Winery

✡ Gan Eden

Blessed art thou, O Lord our God, king of the universe, who blesses the fruit of the vine.

This is the hamotzi:
Ba-ruch atah Adonai elohe-nu melech ha-olam ha-motzi lechem min ha-uretz.

Blessed art thou, O Lord our God, king of the universe, who gives us bread from the earth.

A True Story

Lisa Meyer brought a Baptist friend from the South home for Shabbat dinner one Friday. The friend was very concerned that it might be sacrilegious or offensive for her to eat the challah after the hamotzi. Lisa told her it wasn't like taking communion and the girl felt much better.

Another True Story

"I was dating this Jewish girl. Her parents are Orthodox Jews. Anyway, they invited me over for dinner, and being the gentleman that I am, I brought wine. I walked in the door and with great ceremony, extended my very sophisticated, very expensive bottle of wine to the father. He inspected it closely with great concern on his face. Finally, he looked up at me and said, 'I cannot accept this wine.' 'Why?' I asked, quite stunned. 'It is not kosher,' was the reply. Of course it never occurred to me to check the wine to see if it was kosher. So I took the wine back home and quite enjoyed it.

"A couple of weeks later I went back to their house for dinner. This time I took great pains to find the best kosher wine in the city. Convinced I had the best available kosher wine, and quite certain that I was going to make a big hit, I knocked on the door. With even greater ceremony than the last time I extended my offering to the father. The father gravely took the bottle into his hands and inspected it closely, 'I cannot accept this wine,' he said finally. I thought he was joking. 'Why not?' I asked. 'It is Shabbat. We cannot accept gifts on the Sabbath.'

"So I ended up taking the kosher wine back home and I have to say, it was definitely not as good as the first bottle."   —Richard Morton

CHALLAH

Makes 3 medium-size loaves

This rich, braided egg bread is found at almost every gathering where there is food. And since it wouldn't be a Jewish gathering without food, you come across challah (pronounced "Ha-la") a lot. After the blessing over the bread, rip a hunk off and pass the loaf on to the next person. This, quite obviously, is called breaking bread. It should be called breaking your diet. Challah is extremely fattening, as this recipe illustrates.

9 cups flour
1¹/₄ cup sugar
3 packages dry yeast
1 tablespoon salt
2¹/₂ cups lukewarm water
¹/₂ cup oil
5 eggs
Poppy or sesame seeds

In large bowl, combine 2¹/₂ cups flour, sugar, yeast, salt, water, and oil. Mix well. Add 4 eggs and 1¹/₂ cups flour. Mix well. Add remaining flour, one cup at a time. Mix in between each cup of flour. Knead well. Cover with towel, and let rise for 2–2¹/₂ hours. Divide dough into three parts.

If dough is too sticky to work with, slowly add flour as needed. Braid into three loaves. Beat the remaining egg and brush it onto the loaves. Sprinkle on poppy or sesame seeds. Bake at 350 degrees for 30 minutes.

✡ ✡

The following is the Shehecheyanu prayer. It is said the first time something is done or occurs, whether it is the first time this year or the first time ever. It is also said at the end of Shabbat during the *Havdalah*.

HAVDALAH

Held on Saturday evenings, *havdalah* is a beautiful and intimate ceremony marking the division between *Shabbat* and the regular week. *Havdalah* literally means "separation" in Hebrew. The brief ceremony includes wine, a braided candle, and a spice box filled with fragrant herbs or spices such as cinnamon and nutmeg. As people greet each other on the Sabbath with *Shabbat Shalom* or *Good Shabbes*, the traditional parting words at the end of the havdalah service are *Shavua tov*, meaning "have a good week."

Ba-ruch atah Adonai elohe-nu melech ha-olom sheh-heche-ah-nu ve-ki-yi-mo-nu ve-higi-a-nu laz-man ha-zeh.

Blessed art thou, O Lord our God, King of the universe, who has granted us life, sustained us and enabled us to reach this occasion.

A True Story: Shabbat in the Holy Land with Batman and Robin

"It was our honeymoon. I always imagined going to Bermuda or maybe Hawaii. We, instead, went to Israel. My mother thinks Israel is a land full of crazy people running around doing foreign-type things—like reading backwards and taking a day off during the week and bombing buses and markets and shooting other people's leaders dead and creating a state based on religion. My mother is from West Virginia. But this story isn't about my mother and her opinion of the Jewish state, it's about a WASPy sort of guy going to a Shabbat dinner in the Holy Land.

"My bride, Rachel, had this idea to have Shabbat in Jerusalem with a family. This is a service set up by these two guys (code names 'Batman and Robin,' she told me), from New York who want to recruit young American Jews for aliyah or yeshiva or something my mother would definitely think was very subversive. The deal is that you go to the Wailing Wall at sunset and try to find this guy and he'll hook you up with a family for a real live Shabbat dinner in the holiest of cities on the planet.

"Rachel also informed me that some people end up eating with this guy named Gil. He lives with another guy and they tell stories about their awful, yet fascinating lives (being hippies, fucking Liza Minnelli, being on the cover of *Newsweek*, inventing the hamburger, etc.) and how their search ended when they found Judaism.

"On the way to Batman and Robin, I had to memorize the blessing over the bread and the wine. I had a hard time with Spanish in the seventh grade. So hamotzi lechem min ha-ah-retz tore me apart. Four-year-old boys with sideburns and yarmulkes were looking at me strangely as I sang boreh pri hagufen to the tune of 'Sweet Virginia.' Rachel had informed me that if I went as the gentile I was, the dinner would be a bummer for all since they wouldn't be able to open the wine. She claimed it would be best if I went as an imposter (a Jew) so fun could be had by all.

"Well, when we got to the Wall, Batman and Robin were there. A bunch of people were standing around waiting to be picked. I felt like I was in high school waiting to get on the good team. Finally, we were practically the only people left and Robin said the count was getting full at every house for Shabbat. So Rachel pleaded.

"As a result of her pleading we got to eat Shabbat dinner with Gil. My very first Shabbat dinner. In Israel. With my bride, a nice Jewish kid from Scotland, and Gil.

"After he told us all—a daughter and father from New Jersey, the boy from Scotland (yeshiva bound!), Rachel and I, and a few others—about the trials and tribulations of Gil, he proceeded to give us a lesson and ask us questions.

"He asked my name.

"'My name is Bill.'

"'No, that's your TV name. What's your Hebrew name?'

"Hamotzi? Rachel and I did not go over this. I couldn't think. I got nervous.

"'My mother didn't give me a Hebrew name.'

"After that, Gil didn't like me. He gave me a lecture on my sorry ass state of affairs and that I was a product of TV and I didn't have an original thought in my head.

"In the end, dinner turned out okay, other than being humiliated in front of complete strangers. I mean, after all, I did have Shabbat in the Holy Land, and Rachel and I have been celebrating Shabbat ever since."

—Bill Mackey

POSTMODERN SHABBAT

The Stein family is caught in a strange place between assimilation and observance. They put their TV on a timer so it automatically turns on for shows they like that air on Friday nights and Saturdays. This way they can watch without breaking the Sabbath by turning on the television.

HOLIDAYS TO KNOW ABOUT WHEN DATING A SUPER-JEW

SUKKOTH OR FEAST OF TABERNACLES

Sukkoth (pronounced "sue-coat") is a little bit like Thanksgiving in that it celebrates the harvest. In fact, the Pilgrims supposedly modeled their festival after this biblical harvest feast. The holiday also symbolizes the time when the Israelites wandered in the desert for forty years after their exodus from Egypt. A bonus moral of the holiday is that even if you have a pleasant home, it's good to be reminded of those who are forced to live in poverty. It strengthens character and fends off arrogance.

Celebrated since the time of King Solomon and the First Temple, Jews build temporary booths, or *sukkahs*, that resemble the structures in which the Israelites dwelled while in the desert. Traditionally, Jews moved into their sukkahs for the seven days of Sukkoth. They would move their furniture and beds into the sukkah and use it as their home. Dwelling in the sukkah is a reminder of man's fragile and temporary nature in the universe. Sukkahs always have partially open roofs so you can see the stars and the night sky. This is especially nice as Sukkoth always begins on a full moon.

Hospitality and sharing the bounty of the harvest with others is a basic element of the holiday. Friends and neighbors come round and every night in the sukkah is a party.

PURIM

Strong women are a theme throughout Judaism. Just try to cross your mother-in-law-to-be and you'll see what we mean. Purim (pronounced "poor-um") is the story of Esther, the Jewish queen who saved the Jews in the ancient Persian empire from being massacred in the fifth century B.C.E. The holiday is called Purim because that is the Hebrew word for "lots." To choose which day to massacre the Jews, lots were cast. And the lucky day on which the Jews were to be attacked and killed (but weren't) was the thirteenth day of Adar, which is when the festival is observed.

Here's the story: As a young orphan, Hadassah hung around the court of King Ahasuerus (also known as Xerxes) with her uncle Mordechai, who was an official and also happened to be Jewish. He persuaded her to change her name from Hadassah to Esther and keep her Judaism a secret. Beautiful and smart, Esther caught the eye of the king and soon became his queen. Later, Mordechai refused to kneel before the evil Prime Minister Haman. Haman was furious and got the king to consent to his plot to kill all the Jews. At this time, Jews were not allowed to take up arms. Mordechai insisted that Esther intervene for her people. She summoned her courage and convinced the king to let the Jews defend themselves—Haman was foiled.

Nowadays, Haman's defeat is celebrated carnival-style with the reenactment of the Purim story, read from the *Megillah*, the Scroll of Esther. Dress up in costume—the crazier, the better. Everyone cranks *greggors* (noisemakers) every time Haman's name is spoken. The dessert of choice is *hamantaschen*, a three-cornered pastry said to resemble Haman's hat. Grown-ups are supposed to get drunk. This is the only time that Jews are encouraged to get drunk. And they are supposed to get absolutely schnockered. The idea is to get so inebriated that you can't tell the difference between Haman and Mordechai. To put it in more modern terms, not knowing the difference between Haman and Mordechai is like not knowing the difference between Hitler and Gandhi.

SHEVUOTH

Every May or June, most Jews ignore this seldom-celebrated holiday. Super-Jews know it as the first wheat harvest and the time when God gave Moses the Torah and Ten Commandments. It is surprising that this holiday isn't more recognized—the Mount Sinai event is the most important one in Jewish history. It is the day when the Israelites became Jews. Shevuoth (pronounced "sheh-vu-ess") is sometimes referred to as the Pentecost because it falls on the fiftieth day after the first day of Passover. But who's counting?

Since the early 1800s, Shevuoth has generally been the time when annual confirmation exercises are held in Reform temples.

What better day to welcome young people into the Jewish community than the day Jews became Jews in the first place? During Shevuoth, a medieval Aramaic hymn is chanted in temple. There is a custom of filling the temple and homes with flowers and branches to commemorate the pilgrimages of days gone by. Families traditionally eat blintzes and dairy foods to remind them of God's promise to bring Jews to a land flowing with milk and honey. Dairy foods are also a sign of accepting and following the rules of the Torah, where it says not to boil a kid in its mother's milk (i.e., the kosher laws).

SIMCHAS TORAH

This holiday takes place in mid-fall, the day after Sukkoth ends, and celebrates the final reading of the Torah (it takes a year to read the entire thing). Simchas Torah (pronounced "sim-khess tor-rah") is festive. A procession carrying the Torah circles the temple seven times with dancing, singing, and children marching and waving flags. In Israel, people celebrate by taking Torahs and dancing in the streets late into the night.

TU' B'SHVAT

Tu' B'Shvat (pronounced "too bish-vaht") falls in February and is the new year of the trees. To celebrate, we plant trees—of course. This holiday appeals to earthy people. It is also a popular festival at Jewish day schools because it gives the kids a legitimate—religious even—excuse to get dirty. Many celebrate by planting a tree in Israel. If you want to get in the spirit and plant a tree in Israel, contact the Jewish National Fund.

HOLIDAYS ALMOST NO ONE (IN THE U.S.) CELEBRATES BUT WE MENTION TO BE COMPREHENSIVE

TISHA B'AV

This day of mourning has yet another fast. (You'd think Jews would be very *svelte* after all this fasting.) Tisha B'Av is a national Israeli holiday commemorating the destruction of the First and Second Holy Temples. On this date (the ninth of the month of Av) in 586 B.C.E., the Babylonians sacked the Temple of Solomon (the First Temple). On the same date 655 years later (70 C.E.), the Romans destroyed the Second Temple. Before the Holocaust, these events were considered the two greatest disasters in Jewish history.

YOM HASHOAH

Observed on April 19, this day was established to remember the Holocaust and the 6 million Jews who perished. Throughout Israel two minutes of silence is observed.

YOM HAATZMAUT

Independence Day celebrates the day the State of Israel officially came into existence.

SEFIRAT HAOMER

The counting of the *omer* (sheaf of new barley) starts on the second night of Passover. It continues for forty-nine days. The fiftieth day is Shavuoth.

ASARA BETEVET FAST

This fast marks the beginning of the siege of Jerusalem, which resulted in the destruction of the city and the Holy Temple.

TAANIT ESTHER FAST

This fast day is fairly recent in origin. It commemorates the three days that Queen Esther fasted before approaching King Ahasuerus on behalf of the Jewish people. This day before the Purim festivities is one of abstention. It is a day of solemn remembrance of the near destruction of the Jews at the hand of a Hitler-like villain named Haman.

LAG B'OMER

Literally the thirty-third day of counting the omer between Passover and Shevouth, this is a day of celebration for Israel. During the seven-week period of counting the omer, weddings and popular events are forbidden in remembrance of the plague that killed thousands of students and followers of Rabbi Akiva in the second century. The plague ended on Lag b'Omer. Therefore the ban on festivities is lifted on this holiday.

Another belief is that on this day manna fell from heaven onto the starving Israelites as they wandered the desert. Lag b'Omer also remembers the Hadrianic persecution of the Jews that made Torah study dangerous. It is also observed as the anniversary of the death of Rabbi Simeon ben Yohai, the author of the most sacred book of Jewish mysticism, the *Zohar*. For all of the reasons listed above, Lag b'Omer is known as the Scholar's Holiday. Schoolchildren celebrate by doing things like going on picnics, outings, and having bonfires.

SHEVAESREI BETAMUZ FAST

Commemorates the first breach of the walls surrounding Jerusalem.

MONTH OF ELUL

The final month of the Jewish calendar is a time for introspection and preparing oneself for Rosh Hashanah and the coming year.

Chapter 3

From Bris to Brandeis: Growing Up Jewish

You can benefit from this chapter in two ways. First, you'll learn the rites of passage—both traditional and cultural—for Jewish boys and girls. You may find it good preparation for raising Jewish children in today's society.

But you'll also get a peek into the way your boyfriend was brought up: from a bar mitzvah boy in a plaid suit and braces to teen tour stud to Alpha Epsilon Pi president. Now you'll know where your girlfriend's doting parents came from, and more important, where she's heading. You'll get a picture of just how much of an impact growing up Jewish had on your guy or girl.

FAMILY PLANNING

Having children is the core mitzvah of marriage. Plus, it is said that if you have kids who are good and do good things, your soul benefits. So, if you are having a child, *mazel tov*! If not, get going! What are you waiting for?

According to Judaism, a couple is supposed to re-create itself and therefore have at least two children. Orthodox families, however, believe the more the merrier, sometimes having a child a year. As

"The division between man and woman is not as important as the multiplication."

—GRAND RABBI OF BUCHAREST

THE EVIL EYE

Kineahora (pronounced "kine-ah-hoar-ah") is Yiddish for jinx or bad luck. Jews don't buy baby gifts before the birth out of fear of giving the pregnancy a kineahora.

ABORTION

The fetus is considered to be part of the mother, not a separate entity. Therefore, abortion is not considered murder. In fact, it is required if it will save the mother's life. The mother always comes first in Judaism. Consider your favorite Jewish mother for a moment and you'll know what we mean.

. . . .

one of the most persecuted religious groups—having suffered pogroms, exiles, and the Holocaust—Jews have always felt the need to ensure that the religion will live on in generations to come. On the other hand, you don't see big Reform Jewish families, partly because of their efforts to assimilate to modern American culture. A family with four kids is considered large.

There is only one circumstance when the Bible says it's okay to use birth control: When the pregnancy would be a physical hazard to the mother.

So not being ready or being too busy aren't acceptable excuses for not having kids once you're married (just ask your in-laws). Economic factors should also not affect the choice to use birth control. A man's life is likened to a revolving wheel where he is rich one day and poor the next, or poor one day and rich the next. Better to have children now than wait until the perfect time, since circumstances change.

When birth control is necessary, the act of sex should be conducted as naturally as possible. Methods that put up unnatural blocks to the flow of the life force are not permissible. Think about it. Here's a quick rundown on what is and isn't kosher in the bedroom.

Birth-Control Methods

Acceptable	*Unacceptable*
Oral contraceptives (best)	Abstinence (worst)
Spermicides	Coitus interruptus
Diaphragms	Cervical caps
The rhythm method	Condoms *

PREGNANCY

Whether you're pregnant or you know a knocked-up Jewess, don't plan any baby showers. And put the kibosh on buying presents for the little fetus as well. According to Jewish tradition, it is bad luck to

---

*This is the Jewish position on birth control only. Sexually transmitted diseases and AIDS are not addressed here.

give or buy baby presents before the child is born. God forbid something should happen to the baby or the mother. Never fear—the spoiling will begin the moment the child comes into the world. A world that is filled with Baby Gap, FAO Schwarz, Tiffany's, and, of course, Bloomingdale's.

JEWISH OR NOT?

In the 1980s, the Union of American Hebrew Congregations, the major association of Reform congregations in the United States and Canada, decided that if one parent is Jewish, the child is Jewish. Conservative and Orthodox Jews still go by matriarchal lineage. If the mother is Jewish, so is the kid. If the mother is not Jewish, neither is the kid.

NAMES

Have you ever noticed that there are no Harvey Shapiro IIIs or Joshua Goldbaum Jrs? Children are not named after a living relative because it was believed that the Angel of Death might mistake the younger namesake and summon them to a premature death.

Instead, Ashkenazic Jews of Eastern and Central Europe believe that the dead live on through others' memories of them, so they name their children after deceased relatives. This naming tradition serves to both evoke the qualities possessed by the relative that the parents would like to see in the child as well as pay tribute to the dead relative. Children are not named after siblings that died in childhood or early youth.

Sephardic, or Mediterranean Jews, on the other hand, do not believe in this superstition and often name children after living grandparents.

The rules around naming are pretty loose. All you really need to do is use the same first letter of the relative's name for the child to be considered named after that relative. For example, Eric was named after his great-grandfather Ernest, Jennifer for her grandfather Joseph. It doesn't have to be right on. In this case, it literally is the thought that counts.

JEWISH VIEW ON WHEN LIFE BEGINS

A fetus is not considered a viable human being until after graduation from medical school.

THE JEWISH VIEW ON ANESTHESIA

Go for that epidural, girlfriend! The curse of Eve ("In pain thou give birth") was meant for Eve alone, not her descendants. According to the rabbis, the less pain for the woman, the better.

THE JEWISH GODFATHER

The *sandek* holds the baby boy during the bris. It is a great honor to be asked to hold someone's son while they go under the knife. The parents really trust whomever they ask to fulfill this duty. While they have no role in the child's religious education, the sandek is the closest thing there is to a Jewish godparent.

. . . .

But be forewarned: As you're walking down the aisle, your in-laws and their relatives are already putting in dibs for whom your child should be named. Remember, siblings and cousins are also in contention for honoring the recently deceased by naming their children after them. The family politics can be dicey.

Jewish names change in popularity with generations. Alexanders are named for Abrahams, Rachels for Ruths, Elizabeths for Esthers. Many names just fall by the wayside, like Irving, Melvin, Myron, Florence, and Sadie. Just as well. It's got to be tough being the only Herschel or Ethel among those Ashleys, Emilys, Justins, and Jasons.

Some old-fashioned names are making a comeback in their shortened form, such as Sam, Jake, Ben, Max, and Nate. Some have even switched from male to female, like Sydney and Bari (Barry).

A name also can describe a character trait that the parents desire the child to possess, such as Faith or Rose. Generations ago, girls especially were named after precious metals and gems, just as Jewish last names are: Ruby, Pearl, and Goldie. For the most part, these traditions have faded with the years.

THE BRIS

Almost from his first breath, a Jewish guy's life is different. Eight days after a boy is born, with relatives and family friends looking on, he goes under the knife in the name of God. That's right. You've heard about them, you've even wondered about them, but you've hoped and prayed that you'd never have to go to one—the *bris* (pronounced "briss"), the ritual circumcision. If you do end up attending one, remember the old joke: "Never take a front row seat at a bris."

The service itself is very quick, about five minutes. The little boy also officially gets his Hebrew name here. The cutting of the foreskin is made with one very swift swipe with a very sharp blade. The cut itself causes little actual pain and heals in a couple of days. The parents check to make sure the *mohel** didn't slip and cut off some of

———————————

*Mohel (pronounced "moy-el"): the man who performs the circumcision is usually not a surgeon, but instead a technician whose duties are limited to one quick, clean cut per bris. Many a joke has been made at this poor fellow's expensive. Here's one: "The rabbis get the fees, but the mohels get all the tips."

the baby's manhood. A Band-Aid is put on the tip of the penis. Then it's lox and bagels for everyone!

In truth, the bris is Mommy and Daddy's first party. The food will be plentiful, so be ready to eat.

Having a bris is pretty much a given. If you and your Jewish spouse have a baby boy, even if your spouse rarely participates in other Jewish ceremonies, chances are he or she will want to have a bris. In fact, it's the most practiced ritual in Judaism.

Circumcision

The first circumcision was a pledge between Abraham and God. One of the most sacred commandments, the circumcision symbolizes the covenant between God and Israel. It is a mark of devotion to God at the very source of life.

THE NAMING CEREMONY

In the age of equal rights, a baby girl also gets her own "Welcome to the World" party, called the *simchat bat* (pronounced "sim-khat bot"). This comes by way of a ceremony where she receives her Hebrew name. In keeping with the patriarchal nature of Judaism, the bris is a much bigger deal than the simchat bat is.

The ceremony itself is rather short. Usually the father is called up to read from the Torah, the rabbi says a special prayer for the health and welfare of the mother and child, and the daughter receives her Hebrew name. While this isn't a major religious event, it's an opportunity for the family to see the baby, welcome the child into the Jewish community, and of course, another excuse for a deli tray.

THE JEWISH EDUCATION

Education is a major tenet of Judaism. Studying Torah was once considered the noblest way for a man to spend his life. Jewish women, on the other hand, have always been expected to take care of the

PRAYER SAID AT BRIS OR SIMCHAT BAT

"May the parents rear this child to adulthood imbued with love of Torah and the performance of good deeds, and may they escort him (or her) to the wedding canopy."

IS THAT A BOY OR A GIRL?

Traditionally, a Jewish boy does not cut his hair until the age of three. According to Rabbi Israel Pesach Feinhandler, the reasons behind this practice are cabalistic—that is, from the cabala, Jewish mystical philosophy and practice. And hair is a source of strength, as you'll remember from the story of Samson and Delilah.

GRANDMA'S NACHES

Grandma took little Herbie and Harvey for a walk. They ran into one of Grandma's friends from the temple sisterhood. "Oy. What beautiful grandchildren you have. How old are they?"

"The doctor is three," Grandma explained, "and the lawyer is five."

home. Women were educated to some degree but not allowed to spend their lives as scholars. To find out what life was like for one woman who tried, rent the movie *Yentl*. Barbra is in it. And as always she is amazing.

Study is still heavily promoted among Jews. But the purpose is no longer to be closer to God but instead to get a job that lets you buy closer to the beach.

RELIGIOUS SCHOOL

Much to their displeasure, from the ages of six through sixteen, Jewish kids from observant families spend a weekend morning in religious school. Classes take place in the temple or building annex.

These mornings are spent studying the Torah, singing folk songs, learning about the Jewish holidays, creating art projects, and ingesting enough grape juice, challah, and Tam-Tam* crackers to last a lifetime. It also gives them the chance to socialize with kids in the congregation who attend other schools during the week.

Most of what people know about Judaism is actually picked up in religious school. Israel and current events and how they affect world Jewry are also in the curriculum. If they'd just read this book, they could have saved a lot of weekends.

HEBREW SCHOOL

Any disdain kids might have for religious school pales in comparison to how they feel about Hebrew school. These twice-weekly classes start in the fourth grade and take place after school. This is one of the few places kids are called by their Hebrew names. Kids learn the Hebrew alphabet and basic vocabulary. Unfortunately,

---

*Manishewitz's flat, tasteless crackers. Temples and Jewish day schools feed Tam-Tams to children year-round. They must fear that the eight-day Passover binge didn't satisfy the unleavened bread craving that afflicts so many of our children. If they ever do run short of them, they just cut up a bunch of extra cardboard and serve that. The kids are so hopped up on grape juice anyway they rarely notice.

many people come out of these classes knowing how to read the language but not knowing the translation. All this schooling leads up to the climax: the bar or bat mitzvah near their thirteenth birthday.

BAR MITZVAH

The bar (for boys) or bat (for girls) mitzvah is a milestone in the life of every Jew. It marks the passage from childhood to adulthood. Years of Hebrew school and months of intense bar/bat mitzvah training lead up to this pinnacle Saturday morning. The main event is when the bar mitzvah boy or bat mitzvah girl (yes, those terms are actually used) is called up to the bimah to read the Torah.

The Torah is especially difficult to read because the Hebrew in the actual scroll does not have vowels. (In Hebrew, the vowels are written below and above the letter.) The Torah portion is chanted, so not only is the kid reading in another language, but he or she must also sing each syllable. Chanting the whole portion takes about five minutes. With a preadolescent voice, this feels like an eternity. It's even more nerve wracking if the bar mitzvah is in an Orthodox shul. The Orthodox will not stand for any mistakes. People in the congregation must hear the exact word of God as it was written. So if someone makes a mistake when reading the Torah in an Orthodox shul, a bunch of old men will usually start making noise to cover up the mistake. Then the reader must stop and reread the line correctly.

In locales with high concentrations of Jews, bar mitzvahs dominate junior high school social schedules. They keep parents pretty busy as well. Sometimes parents attend the bar mitzvah. Other times they just get to carpool back and forth to various events. The service, while the religious reason for the bar mitzvah, is just the tip of the iceberg.

To most, the bar mitzvah is actually an excuse to throw a party. Many bar mitzvah parties rival wedding receptions. They can be luncheons or evening affairs. The magnitude of the event really depends on the child's family and their finances. Many parents see it as an opportunity to entertain their friends, family, and business associates. Some kids even get two parties—one for relatives and parents' friends, known as the "grown-up party," and one for their friends.

"If you want to recapture your youth, just cut off his allowance."

—AL BERNSTEIN[*]

[*]From *On Good Advice* by William Safire (New York: Random House Value Publishing, 1943)

INTERFAITH CHILD REARING

Two lawyers, Joe Deluca and Elaine Katzman, got married. When people ask them how they are raising their kids, they say, "Very guilty." They go on to say that they have thought of doing a controlled experiment of raising one child Catholic and one Jewish and seeing which came out more screwed up. We think they're kidding, but you never know.

. . . .

For a child, a bar mitzvah is like the ultimate dream birthday party. Often there are large centerpieces on the tables themed to the kid's favorite activities or interests. There are huge balloon clusters everywhere. Some even have things like monogrammed mints, "Ronnie's bar mitzvah, February 6, 1982" napkins, and chocolate-covered Oreo cookies. And those are just the table decorations.

There is also entertainment. The parents hire a band or DJ. This is often kids' first introduction to coed dancing. Next time you're at a Jewish event, whether a wedding or charity where there is dancing, call out "Snowball" during one of the slow songs. It's sure to get some laughs as well as stir up some adolescent memories of sweaty palms, stepping on toes, and pubescent crushes. Usually nothing too steamy goes on, as the bar mitzvah boy is still young enough that his parents might also hire magicians, tumblers, and such to spice up the party. Obviously, this mode of celebration is a modern phenomenon and has little to do with what the ceremony is all about.

GOING TO A BAR/BAT MITZVAH?

When in doubt, savings bonds make the perfect gift. If you want to appear really in the know, buy Israeli bonds (which invest in such industries as shipping, chemicals and minerals, power stations, housing, road construction, etc.). Other popular gifts are stock, cash, and fancy pens.

In the eyes of the bar mitzvah boy, all of the attention and celebration usually pales in comparison to the gifts he receives for being bar mitzvah'd. Ask your friends what they did with their bar mitzvah money way back in the eighties or early nineties. It's probably worth a few laughs. At the very least, you'll learn something. Here are some that were popular:

Immediate Expenditures	*Delayed (due to parental influence)*
Stock market (with help from Mom and Dad)	Buy a car
Computer equipment	Teen trip to Europe or Israel
A boom box	College spending money
Video games	

Some men who become more religious later on in life or women who were not allowed to be bat mitzvah'd (only confirmed, see below) choose to be bar mitzvah'd as adults, as did Kirk Douglas and Henry Winkler (aka The Fonz). They say it is a very moving and meaningful experience, but they usually forgo the big parties, balloons, DJ, and gifts.

CONFIRMATION

During the spring of their sophomore year of high school, Jewish kids finally graduate from religious school. This custom is called Confirmation or "being confirmed." It's not a particularly important milestone. However, those being confirmed are thrilled to regain ownership of their weekend mornings after ten years of forced religious study.

YOUTH GROUP

To keep the teen connected with the temple post–bar mitzvah and -Confirmation, most congregations have fairly large youth groups. Most have a twentysomething-year-old leader who plans activities with the help of more active members. Typical activities are trips to amusement parks, canned-food drives, charity car washes, weekend retreats, dances with other youth groups, and the occasional havdalah service. Many of the teens involved participate because it reminds them of their overnight camp.

SUMMER CAMP

The Jewish camp experience can begin early on with day camps organized by the synagogue or local Jewish Community Center (JCC) for younger kids. When they reach the fifth or sixth grade, kids are shipped off to overnight camp for one or two months with all their worldly belongings packed neatly into a steamer trunk. Yep. A trunk. God knows why.

Jewish camps pretty much run the gamut where levels of observance are concerned. On one end, there are camps that only differ

WHY YOU DON'T SEE MANY FAMOUS JEWISH SPORTS LEGENDS

Jews are very protective of their children. You do not see many Jewish boys going out for high-contact sports like football and hockey. They are encouraged to go out for the tennis team instead. Maybe it's because their doctor and dentist parents saw the injuries that come along with these sports.

Some Jewish men claim that this overprotection caused them to become risk-takers when they got older and were out from under the watchful eyes of their parents. Maybe that's why so many Jews experiment with drugs in their teenage years.

from other overnight camps in that the campers are predominantly Jewish. On the other end are camps that have daily services and intensive Hebrew and Torah study thrown in with classic camp activities like sailing, horseback riding, and archery.

Jewish camps often are coed. If not, they have brother/sister camps nearby. If your friends went to a Jewish camp, chances are this is where they got to second base for the first time. And we don't mean baseball.

A True Story (Summer Camp: A Rite of Passage)

"All good Jews (and for that matter not-so-good Jews) from the East Coast go to summer camp. The 'more Jewish' Jews go to the highly religious summer camps where everyone speaks Hebrew and goes to services daily—just the kind of thing most young Jews want to avoid. For the rest of us, we smatter along the many Jewish summer camps from the Pocono Mountains of Pennsylvania up through the Catskills of New York.

"For eight summers, I went to Camp Pinemere in the Poconos. Being Jewish at our camp simply meant eating kosher meals and attending Friday night and Saturday morning services. The food was so terrible that not mixing milk and meat did not seem like a real big drawback. For instance, PB&J—a staple to replace whatever else was being served—could be supplemented with milk. And if there was a mystery meat for dinner, ample bug juice* would hold you over until canteen ('camp speak' for the onsite store where you could buy candy, chips, and other goodies not provided by the camp).

"Services were a whole different story at Pinemere. The only Hebrew uttered was during the singing of traditional songs. The rest of the ceremony was a cross between a James Taylor concert and an appreciation of nature as lectured by a rabbi wanna-be. White was the standard uniform

---

*Bug juice: A Kool-Aid-like drink that was watered down or not diluted enough, but always tasted vile. Since there was no dairy in the bug juice, it was always served with meat meals.

for services. I have no idea how this tied into the Jewish theme, but at that age we wore what we were told. Overall, services at camp did little to reinforce my sense of Jewishness, but they were a great opportunity to hang out with your cabin-mates and check out the guys.

"That said, these services and the prayers uttered before and after meals are etched in my memory, enabling me to sing along at the Passover seder and Yom Kippur services. This gives my mother great pleasure, though I don't think she was ever duped into believing that the religious aspect was a fundamental part of the camp experience.

"Most everyone who went to Pinemere was Jewish. I'm not really sure how that gave us more or less a sense of belonging, but it was my earliest exposure to being with people en masse of the same religious background. I loved the camp experience, and stayed until my parents forced me to take a job (by then I was eighteen, and it was time to move on).

"To this day, one thing that's high on my list of importance in raising my children (other than not acting like my parents) is to send them to summer camp. There's no replacement for this wonderful experience. I don't know if it's sending them to a Jewish summer camp that's so important or just that all Jews stress such importance on going to summer camp that we all end up together at the same place. Whatever the case, they seem to go hand-in-hand, and it's an invaluable piece of information for anyone dating a Jew to understand."

—Valerie Syme

THE TEEN TOUR

Many moneyed Jewish teens get to go on teen tours. This is a great way to spend the summer for kids too old for overnight camp. There are teen tours to Europe and to areas in the United States, but the most popular destination is Israel. Every summer, thousands of American teens descend upon the Promised Land they have heard so much about in religious school. They visit *kibbutzim*, the Western Wall, and Masada. Of course, all these amazing sights don't compare to the education they receive in getting to know the opposite sex.

TEEN TOUR MEMORIES

Karyn Detje fondly remembers her cross-country trip on a teen tour. "We went from New York to California. It was an eight-week camping trip. Every girl brought a blow dryer."

TATTOOS AND PIERCING

With the exception of earrings for women, any sort of body mutilation or permanent marking is not generally accepted. You just don't see *L'chaim* tattoos and Star of David nose rings. Parents may try to reason with a son or daughter returning to the house with a new tattoo or piercing by saying "it's against our religion." More often than not, that will soon give way to a hearty stream of Yiddish and English expletives, as well as "Are you trying to give me a heart attack?" and "God forbid your grandmother should find out. It could kill her." The thinking behind this is that the body is a holy vessel. God created us in his image. We shouldn't mess with it.

═══════════════════════════════

JEWISH GEOGRAPHY

"A Jew is forever surrounded, if not shielded, by his community, both physically and spiritually."

—ELIE WIESEL,
FROM *A JEW TODAY*

Did you ever notice how all Jews seem to know each other or at least know a lot of the same people? When two Jews meet, there is usually an instant rapport. You've heard of six degrees of separation—where everyone is connected through a chain of six or less people. Between Jews, it's more like two degrees. Camp, youth groups, and teen tours greatly contribute to the phenomenon known as Jewish Geography. Rare is the game of Jewish Geography that doesn't unearth at least one "Ohmigod! I can't believe you went to [fill in camp, teen tour, or college] with them! My family used to spend [fill in holiday] with them every year!"

═══════════════════════════════

WE'RE GOING TO MI-AAAA-MI!

Your family might have stopped taking vacations together after you outgrew Disneyland. This is not the case with Jewish families. Jews take their kids on vacation until the grandkids start driving.

The typical timing is, of course, Christmas. Not for religious reasons, but because they can be in warm weather while their friends back home are freezing their *tuchises* off. They also visit the grandparents:

Spring forward.

Fall back.

Winter in Florida.

COLLEGE

A person really starts to understand what it means to be a Jew when they go to college. For many this is the first time they are around so many non-Jews and that their minority status is illustrated. Fellow students may never have met a Jew before going to college. The young Jewish adult may embrace this newfound freedom and anonymity by not observing the holidays as was done in their parents' house.

On the other hand, Jews coming from more secular areas might be surprised to find themselves searching out Hillel (the on-campus Jewish community) and friends to celebrate the holidays with, as well as exploring the Jewish culture.

LOANS, SCHMOANS

Jews tend to pay for their children's education. Rare is the Jew who takes out a student loan. It is practically unheard of for an undergrad. For grad school, the Jew might get a little public assistance but usually Daddy just covers it all. It is not until the young Jew gets his or her first real job that they are off the family payroll.

Here are some schools with sizable Jewish populations. Please note that the nicknames may seem anti-Semitic, but were given by Jews themselves.

1. BRANDEIS UNIVERSITY, WALTHAM, MASSACHUSETTS: Any Jewish child who attends Brandeis is sure to make his or her parents proud. Brandeis, founded in 1948, is the first Jewish-sponsored non-sectarian university in the Western Hemisphere. However, be aware that the university accepts students on the basis of academic achievement without reference to race or religious affiliation.

2. EMORY UNIVERSITY, ATLANTA, GEORGIA: Probably the only university in the South besides Tulane where there is a strong Jewish contingent.

3. YALE UNIVERSITY, NEW HAVEN, CONNECTICUT: Well, at least compared to Harvard.

Rabbi Judah says: Whoever does not teach his son a trade or profession teaches him to be a thief.

—BABYLONIAN TALMUD, *KIDDUSHIN 29a*

Naches (pronounced "knock-us")—the joy that parents derive from seeing their kids grow up to be happy, mature, productive adults. Just imagine the parental joy when the child graduates from medical or law school.

• • • • • • • • • • • • • • • • • • • •

4. UNIVERSITY OF PENNSYLVANIA, PHILADELPHIA, PENNSYLVANIA: This top-notch school is labeled "the Jewish Ivy."

5. NEW YORK UNIVERSITY, NEW YORK, NEW YORK: Needless to say, there are a lot of Jews in New York.

6. BOSTON UNIVERSITY, BOSTON, MASSACHUSETTS: Often referred to as "B. Jew" rather than BU, this school attracts students from the tri-state area (New York, New Jersey, and Pennsylvania) in droves.

7. Tulane University, New Orleans, Louisiana: Some call it "Jew-lane." At one point in the nineties, it was even 30 percent Jewish.

With college come Jewish fraternities and sororities. A few are Alpha Epsilon Pi (AEPi), Zeta Beta Tau (ZBT), Alpha Epsilon Phi (AEPhi), and Sigma Delta Tau (SDT). Although miles away from their homes, students still feel obligated to make the grades. As heard in *Animal House*: "We're in trouble. I just checked with the guys at the Jewish house, and they said that every one of our answers on the psych test was wrong."

You can only give so much credit to the parents, the summer camp, the teen tour, and the education. . . . "The final forming of a person's character lies in their own hands" (Anne Frank).

Chapter 4

Have a Little More Brisket, Darling: Food Is Love

Brisket, blintzes, kreplach, knishes. Chicken soup, kugel, *rugelach.* Bagels and lox, bagels and cream cheese, bagels and whitefish from Zabar's.* Matzah ball soup. A Rueben on rye.** Nathan's hot dogs. Kosher dill pickles. Potato latkes. These are a few of our favorite things.

Jews love food. Jews eat a lot. And often. All holidays revolve around eating, except Yom Kippur, which is all about *not* eating. Either way you slice it, Jews obsess about food.

Jewish food is heavy, rich, stick-to-your-ribs kind of food. If you're on a diet, you'd better check it at the door. One round at the Break the Fast buffet or first course of a wedding dinner will end that notion.

Marilyn Brody's prized kugel isn't for the faint of heart. "One piece," she whispers sinfully, "is like eating a stick of butter." You could rack up several sticks during a good holiday meal. Jewish mothers used to cook with oil, butter, schmaltz—ingredients any self-respecting person would cringe at using now.

Hamotzi is the Hebrew word for "brings forth." It is a key word in the blessing before meals. Instead of referring to the prayer said before eating as "grace" Jews say the hamotzi. See the holiday chapter for the words to the hamotzi.

---

*Zabar's: a famous Jewish deli/gourmet food store in New York.
**Corned beef and/or pastrami, sauerkraut, spicy brown mustard and Thousand Island dressing jammed between two thick slices of rye bread—a recipe for heartburn.

FLYING KUGEL

Halley Porter (not a Jew, if you couldn't tell by the name) worked for a while as a waitress at a Jewish deli in Chevy Chase, Maryland. One day, an old man came in and asked her if they had any kugel. Halley thought the word *kugel* sounded famil-iar, but she couldn't put her finger on exactly what it was. So, thinking she had a safe answer, she replied in her perkiest voice, "Why, yes sir! It's flown in fresh every day!"

. . . .

THE VERY BEST KUGEL RECIPE
Yield 10 servings

There are pros and cons to the recipe below. On the one hand, you can't kid yourself that it's not that bad for you. And after tasting it, people will be constantly hounding you to make it. On the other hand, you now have a dish that you can be proud to serve to the most Jewish of palettes. Please note that you must prepare this a day in advance, as it must be refrigerated overnight before cooking. It can be eaten cold but it's much better hot.

16-ounce package noodles
Two 8-ounce packages of cream cheese
$1/_2$ pound butter or margarine
3 cups milk
1 cup sugar
8 eggs (beaten well)
2 teaspoons vanilla
Cornflake crumbs, cinnamon and sugar for topping

Cook and drain noodles. Set aside. Melt cream cheese and butter in large saucepan. Add milk and sugar and continue to stir until dissolved. It should have the consistency of light custard. Remove from stove. Add beaten eggs and vanilla. Mix with cooked noodles. Pour into a 9x13-inch greased pan. There will be some left over that doesn't fit in the pan. Put this in a smaller pan.

Refrigerate overnight.

Put crumbs, cinnamon, and sugar on top before cooking. Bake at 400 degrees for 15 minutes. Reduce heat to 375 degrees and cook for 30 more minutes. Serve hot.

Gone are the *zaftig* women of our grandmother's time. Today's Jewish woman, whether she is a suburban matron or a city girl, is much more slender. After generations of cholesterol bingeing, we're a little more selective about our calories.

THE EVOLUTION OF THE BAGEL

One carryover from our caloric past is bagels. The best bagels, if you haven't heard already, are made in New York City. Maybe it's the seasoned bakers harking back to Old World recipes that make them better; maybe it's the famous New York water. Either way, you haven't really had a good bagel until you bite into one in the Big Apple. Some former New Yorkers even have their bagels overnighted from New York to their homes in Los Angeles, Chicago, or wherever. This is a bit extreme.

Once upon a time you had a nice respectable variety of bagels: plain, egg, poppy, sesame, and cinnamon raisin. Now, they have hit the mainstream and gotten out of control. There are bagel stores on every corner in almost every city from Manhattan to Des Moines. They're baking flavors of bagels and smearing cream cheese that would make Grandma Goldie's hair stand on end: strawberry, blueberry, sun-dried tomato basil, jalapeno, even chocolate chip. Oy!

Many Jews stand on principle that fruity bagels—your strawberries, blueberries, and cherries—are a faux pas, and it is an affront to bring them to any Jewish-eating event. They don't mix well with cream cheese or butter, and you certainly couldn't lay a half dozen slices of corned beef on one. So what good are they? Remember this mantra when it's your turn to bring the bagels for Sunday brunch: No fruity bagels!

Then there's the bagel-scooping phenomenon, which is prevalent in New York delis and Boca Raton clubhouses. There are people out there who (with their fingers even) scoop out the doughy part of a bagel and spread their cream cheese or scrambled egg whites in the hollowed-out remains. This way it's supposed to be less caloric. Don't ask. It's a Jewish thing. And for the record, don't serve thawed Lender's Bagels. Enough said.

DELIS

Long, long ago, when Jews lived in working-class sections of cities and money was scarce, the woman of the house would cook large meals showcasing the dishes of their homelands: Russia, Poland,

Ila Abramson brought her non-Jewish boyfriend to meet her mother at a local deli. Nate ordered a blueberry bagel with cream cheese and tomato. Ila's mother promptly leaned over and whispered in her daughter's ear, "Omigawd. Your grandmother is rolling over in her grave."

JACKIE MASON'S VIEW ON JEWISH FOOD (AND HE SHOULD KNOW!)

"Chicken soup, for Jews, is what pizza, frankfurters, and apple pie all together are for gentiles."

"Countries are compared to chopped liver, women are compared to chopped liver, shirts are compared to chopped liver. It's the only word in the world that everything is compared to. You never have to worry about saying it out of place. It's always in place."

Jackie Mason, *How to Talk Jewish* (New York: St. Martin's Press, 1990).

Germany, Austria, and so on. Recipes for these foods were passed down through the generations and usually only make an appearance at holiday tables and delis.

Delicatessens are the mainstays of hearty Jewish fare. Here you'll learn it all starts with the bread: light rye, dark rye, marble rye, pumpernickel, onion rolls, and challah. Never plain white bread! You need a sturdy foundation to support three inches of corned beef, sauerkraut, and Thousand Island dressing. No wonder white bread is shunned.

Here's a glossary of deli delights. Clip and save for easy access.

✡ Bialy (be-ah-lee): A slightly flatter bagel without the hole and grilled onion sprinkled on top.

✡ Blintzes: Crepes filled with blueberries or sweet cheese.

✡ Borscht: This ominous-looking red beet soup, usually served cold with a dollop of sour cream, has its roots in Russia.*

✡ Cheesecake: The downfall of any dieter. New York, of course, has the best, and entire restaurants have been dedicated to this sinful dessert.

✡ Chicken soup: A delicious broth chockfull of vegetables and more often than not egg noodles. This potent brew, grandmothers far and wide claim, has mystical medicinal values. Try it for yourself.

✡ Chopped liver: You guessed it. Or smelled it. It's an acquired taste.

✡ Cream soda and flavored seltzers: Aids in digestion.

✡ Egg creams: No egg, no cream. Just syrup, seltzer, and milk— explain that one. You'll have to go to an old-fashioned diner to find this paradox.

✡ Gefilte fish: Jews in Eastern Europe who couldn't afford a whole fish would grind up pieces of leftover fish and pack it together. Today, it comes in a nice glass jar brought to us by the good people at Manischewitz. If you want to get really fancy, you can also buy it fresh at better Jewish delis.

---

*This soup lent its name to the resort area of the Catskill Mountains in New York, which had almost exclusively Jewish patrons. Traveling stand-up comedians of the forties and fifties performed here and made the Borscht Belt famous.

✿ Kishka (kish-kah): A sausagelike food, actually stuffed intestines.*

✿ Knish: Large dumplings filled with potato, minced meat, or spinach.**

✿ Kosher dill: A large tasty pickle served with a sandwich or just in a bowl on the table. Enjoy it now and later, since the flavor will stay on your breath all day long.

✿ Kosher frank: A beef hot dog with all good, fresh ingredients, as opposed to regular frankfurters, which can be made from question-able or old animal parts.

✿ Kreplach (krep-lahck): Dumplings with chopped meat or cheese usually in soup. Think wontons.

✿ Latkes: Deliciously greasy potato pancakes served with sour cream or applesauce (see page 54 for recipe).

✿ Lox: Smoked salmon, served on bagels with cream cheese or on a platter. Really make an impression by knowing the difference between nova (without salt) and regular (salty).

✿ Matzah ball soup: Chicken broth with carrots, celery, and a large ball of matzah meal.***

✿ Nosh: Not a food but a verb. It's what you do at a deli or right from your fridge to tide you over until the next meal.

✿ Pastrami: cured meat. The fattier the tastier. Pile it on rye with spicy brown mustard.

✿ Rugelach: Flaky cookies with raspberry, nut, or chocolate centers.

✿ Schmear: What you do with cream cheese and other spreads.

✿ Spicy brown mustard: Whatever you do, don't put ketchup on your deli sandwich.

✿ Spreads: What you put on bagels. Whitefish spread, lox spread, and chopped liver are traditional. Sun-dried tomato basil, strawberry, and honey walnut cream cheeses are neo-Jewish.

✿ Stuffed cabbage: An ominous-looking and -smelling Russian dish.

✿ Whitefish: smoked whole or in a spread.

---

*So when someone says he got kicked in the kishkas, you know what he means.
**"What's a 'nish'?" explained the sign posted in Kupel's Bakery in Brookline, Massachusetts, to save the noninitiated customer from certain embarrassment.
***It takes years of practice to get matzah balls fluffy. One wrong move and you have a mass that looks and tastes like a bowling ball.

Michael Dash's favorite memory of holiday dinners in old New York was of the glass bottles of seltzer. These, made famous by Clarabel the Clown, were served with meals because the bubbles aided digestion (think Alka-Seltzer). Although he no longer eats cholesterol-laden foods, Michael still buys Dr. Brown's and other old-fashioned sodas for the bubble effect.

When Jews moved out of the city ghettos to the gentrified neighborhoods and suburbs, they stumbled upon the answer to all their prayers: restaurants. There is one surefire way to recognize the Jews in a restaurant. They are boisterous and complain loudly that the service is bad, that their filet isn't perfectly pink inside, and that their table is too close to the kitchen. They are also the first ones to compliment the chef on a good meal and will explain in great detail about other excellent meals they've had elsewhere. They are not shy about calling across the room—"Yoohoo!"—to a fellow diner they recognize.

You'll learn that restaurants are perfect places to make a scene, which this woman did recently. According to witnesses: A tall, blond woman loudly ticked off the reasons why she was breaking up with her Jewish boyfriend, culminating with these carefully articulated words as she stormed out of the restaurant, "And I'm tired of being called a shiksa!"

Jews are also the ones who eat off someone else's plates. So don't be taken aback if your boyfriend's sister spears one of your potatoes without batting an eye. Chalk it up to loving food. Jews want to taste everything. If it's on the table, it's up for grabs. This could be why we have such an affinity for Chinese food. Not only is it fast and cheap but there's guaranteed variety. Also, Chinese restaurants are conveniently open on Christmas. For Jews, Christmas dinner means going out for Chinese food.

According to Jewish dietary law, pork and shellfish may be eaten only in Chinese restaurants, preferably in fried rice. Well, not exactly, but it sure seems that way. Especially on Sunday nights, you'll find Chinese restaurants across the country packed with Jews. In some towns and neighborhoods, they serve as impromptu meeting places. What Jews probably like best is that no matter how much Chinese food you eat, you'll be noshing two hours later.

THE JEWISH STOMACH PHENOMENON

If you've ever eaten a full—and we mean *full*—Jewish meal, you'll notice your stomach starts to take on a life of its own. It gurgles, it talks, it emits strange odors. It's official: You're on your way to a Jewish stomach.

Although tasty, Jewish food sits like a rock in your gut. Don't worry. At least three people within shouting distance will be carrying a month's supply of Pepto Bismol, Maalox, or Milk of Magnesia. Be prepared for some probing questions though. "Are you feeling a little gassy, darling? You don't look so good." Don't be shy. Discuss your symptoms in gory detail. Really. Someone else at the table will be sure to jump in with stories of their stomach woes.

KOSHER LAWS

If Jews had a cardinal sin (besides paying full retail) it would be ordering a ham and cheese in a deli. This little sandwich flies in the face of the Jewish kosher laws for two reasons: (1) Pigs are not fit to eat because they carry disease. (2) The Torah tells us not to eat milk products and meat together. Confused? Here are the basics:

Kosher essentially means "fit to eat." Most think of it as being all about cleanliness. Back in the time of Moses, disease was rampant because of unsanitary conditions and spoiled food. The kosher dietary laws helped keep people from getting sick.

Kosher laws also have purposes beyond health considerations; believe it or not, they are supposed to prevent people from polluting their souls. The laws were created to:

✡ Limit the number of animals the Jew can kill and eat.
✡ Make the slaughter of animals as painless as possible.
✡ Cause revulsion at bloodshed.
✡ Instill self-discipline.
✡ Help sustain the Jewish religion and create a cohesive Jewish community.
✡ Elevate the act of eating from an animal-like level to a mini-religious experience.

The separation of milk and meat stems from the biblical warning not to boil a calf in its mother's milk. Jews believe in separating life from death: milk symbolizes life, meat represents death.

Two Jewish men were talking between themselves in Yiddish in a deli frequented almost exclusively by Jews. A Chinese waiter comes up to the table and, in fluent and impeccable Yiddish, asks them if everything is okay, can he get them anything, and so forth.

The men are dumbfounded. "My God, where did he learn such perfect Yiddish?" they both think. After they pay the bill, they ask the deli owner, an old friend also fluent in Yiddish, "Where did your waiter learn such fabulous Yiddish?"

The owner looks around and whispers, "Shhhh. He thinks we're teaching him English."

"What else, I ask you, were all those prohibitive dietary rules and regulations all about to begin with, what else but to give us little Jewish children practice in being repressed . . . takes a dedicated and self-sacrificing parent and a hard-working attentive little child to create in only a few years' time a really constrained and tight-ass human being. Why else the two sets of dishes?"

—PHILIP ROTH,
PORTNOY'S COMPLAINT

Milk and meat must not be consumed at the same time. This means in the same sitting, not merely in the same mouthful or dish. One is supposed to allow six hours for digestion between milk and meat meals. Kosher households keep separate dishes and silverware for the two meals. Some even have two kitchen areas. Others feel confident that today's super-hot dishwashers make it possible to stick with one set of dishes.

If your sweetheart's family keeps kosher, it'll be a lot harder for you. If dating were a video game, you'd be playing at the advanced level. This will help you figure it out:

✡ Three types of kosher food: dairy *(milchig)*, meat *(fleishig)*, and neutral foods like vegetables, grains, fruits, and eggs *(pareve)*. Pareve is like Switzerland in a kosher kitchen—that is it's neither dairy nor meat. Vegetables and grains can be eaten with milk or meat.

✡ Glass (if kept cold) can be used for milk or meat dishes. All metals absorb impurity so in a kosher home, metal pots and pans have to be one or the other. If glass gets hot, things stick to it. No longer pure.

✡ Koshering meat is the additional soaking, salting, and rinsing that are done even after the meat is purchased to drain away any traces of blood that might have remained after the slaughter.

✡ Eating the sciatic nerve is not kosher. Rather than removing it, most kosher butchers don't sell the hindquarters. This is believed to have originated from the biblical story of Jacob who was wounded on the thigh during his struggle with the angel.

Of course, many Jews like to trip up their gentile friends: Rachel Kanter's father used to tell her non-Jewish boyfriends that keeping kosher is just another scam to sell more pots and pans.

Eating out with someone who keeps kosher can be an adventure. Julie O'Malley says of her experiences, "I have learned to throw around kosher terms while ordering Thai food, like chicken in coconut milk. 'Don't worry. That's pareve.'"

ODE TO MARGARINE

You might think margarine is just a by-product of the 1970s. For people who keep kosher, however, it's the best thing to come around since nondairy creamer. Margarine opened up new worlds for the kosher cook. Butter can never be used when meat is on the menu. Margarine, on the other hand, isn't dairy and can be used in recipes and on the table.

When Benji Segal was three years old, he just loved ham. Couldn't get enough of it. This food fetish pained his parents, who were embarrassed to be feeding him the epitome of *trayft* (nonkosher) foods. They were panicked that people would find out, so they told Benji that the food he loved so much was called "cheese."

One day, Benji's grandparents asked him what he wanted to eat. He knew what he wanted: "Cheese!" Happy to oblige, they gave him a hunk of cheese. Much to their surprise, Benji spit it out. Later that day, they took Benji for a walk around the neighborhood. When they passed the butcher shop, Benji stopped and screamed "Cheese!" and pointed with delight at the ham hanging in the window.

Ideally, the Jewish diet should be vegetarian. It's healthier and cuts down on killing animals. However, the kosher laws acknowledge that sometimes you've just got to have some meat. But there is a very limited kosher selection. Certain meats are off-limits, forty-two in fact. Only four-footed animals that chew their cud and have split hooves may be eaten. Chickens and turkeys are okay. So are fish that have fins and scales. No birds of prey, no shellfish, no animals that crawl. And pigs are definitely out. Keep in mind that people who don't keep kosher may still have some aversion to pork. For example, every meal Jeff's Catholic grandmother ever served his Jewish wife, Beth, involved ham or pork as the main course. Beth is convinced she did it on purpose.

The purpose behind all the kosher laws was kindness to animals and health concerns. Not being able to indiscriminately kill animals shows a respect for God's creatures. For animals that can be killed for food, the way the animal is slaughtered is very important. A reli-

DIALOGUE AT MOUNT SINAI

GOD: *And remember, Moses, never cook a calf in its mother's milk.*

MOSES: *Ohhhhhh! So you are saying we should never eat milk and meat together.*

GOD: *No. What I'm saying is, never cook a calf in its mother's milk.*

MOSES: *Oh, Lord, forgive my ignorance! What you are really saying is we should wait six hours after eating meat to eat milk so the two are not in our stomachs at the same time.*

GOD: *No, Moses, what I'm saying is, don't cook a calf in its mother's milk!*

MOSES: *Oh, Lord! Please don't strike me down for my stupidity! What you mean is we should have a separate set of dishes for milk and meat and if we make a mistake we have to bury that dish outside.*

GOD: *Moses, do whatever the fuck you want.*

gious slaughterer first inspects the animal for signs of disease or abnormalities; if it passes, he slashes its throat with one stroke. It is forbidden to eat the meat of an animal that has died by other means, because it would be cruel and/or could be unsanitary. It is also trayft to kill a pregnant animal or to eat an egg with a spot of blood on it.

The meat has to be preserved in a special way—dried and salted. This helped keep foods from spoiling in the days before we had refrigerators and freezers.

Packaged goods have symbols on them if they are kosher. A *U* within a circle ((ⓤ)) means that it follows Jewish dietary laws according to the Union of Orthodox Jewish Congregations of America, the national association of Orthodox congregations. A *K* means that it has been deemed kosher but doesn't say by whose authority.

You may have also seen "Kosher for Passover" on food packages. This means the item doesn't have any yeast or ingredients that are forbidden during the Passover holiday, when Jews don't eat bread or anything that rises.

What would a chapter devoted to food be without a few recipes? Man cannot live on kugel alone, so if the kugel recipe earlier wasn't enough for you, try some of these.

COLD BEET BORSCHT
Serves 10

This soup is a Russian specialty.

> *4 pounds beets, washed and trimmed*
> *salt*
> *2 tablespoons lemon juice*
>
> OPTIONAL GARNISH
> *4 hard-boiled eggs*
> *scallions*
> *cucumbers*
> *sour cream*
> *yogurt*

Cover beets with lightly salted water and bring to a boil. Lower heat and simmer until the beets are tender. As soon as the beets are cool enough, rub off skins. Slice, grate, or julienne and return to cooking liquid. Add lemon juice. Garnish as desired. Serve chilled.

BRISKET WITH SWEET POTATOES AND PRUNES
Serves 8

The sweet-potato-and-prune combination is a variation on tzimmes, a traditional dish.

> 1 first-cut brisket
> 2–3 tablespoons oil
> 1 cup each chopped celery, onion, and carrot
> 1 teaspoon cinnamon
> $^1/_4$ teaspoon nutmeg
> pinch of allspice
> 1 14$^1/_2$-oz can beef stock
> 2 pounds sweet potatoes, sliced 1 inch thick
> 1 $^1/_2$ pounds parsnips, sliced 1 inch thick
> 1 cup pitted prunes
> 1 cup apple cider
> salt and pepper
> chopped parsley for garnish

Brown the meat in the oil. Remove. Add to the pan celery, onion, carrot, and spices. Sauté until brown. Put back the meat. Add the stock. Cook covered in oven at 325 degrees for 1$^1/_2$ hours. Add sweet potatoes, parsnips, and prunes. Continue to cook uncovered until sweet potatoes and parsnips are done. This could take a while. (Briskets are better the longer they are cooked. The meat should be falling apart before it is served.) Remove meat, celery, onion, and carrots. Discard as much fat as possible. Add cider. Return meat to pan to reheat. Add salt and pepper to taste and garnish with parsley.

JEWS WERE THE FIRST ANIMAL RIGHTS ACTIVISTS

Well, activist might not be the proper term, but Jews have always tried to do right by God's fellow creatures:

✡ Jews don't hunt for sport. Animals can only be killed for food or to conduct research that will aid humanity.

✡ A farmer must feed his livestock before sitting down for a meal himself.

✡ Jews just recently started owning pets. Formerly, it was believed that confining an animal in a home was contrary to the natural order.

CHOCOLATE CHALLAH BREAD PUDDING
Serves 10

A great use for day-old challah.

> *1 ¹/₂ cups whole milk*
> *2 cups heavy cream*
> *6 tablespoons sugar*
> *pinch of salt*
> *12 ounces semisweet chocolate, broken up (or chocolate chips)*
> *¹/₂ teaspoon vanilla*
> *3 eggs, beaten*
> *3 cups cubed challah (preferably stale)*
> *butter*

Combine milk, cream, sugar, salt, and chocolate and heat on low until chocolate is melted. Add vanilla. Remove from heat. Whisk in eggs. Add challah and coat well. Refrigerate 2–3 hours, stirring occasionally. Bake at 350 degrees in a buttered soufflé dish for 40 minutes until tester comes out dry. Serve warm.

CHOCOLATE CHIP MERINGUES
Yield one dozen

Note: This is a good dessert for Passover because there isn't any yeast or flour in it. If serving during Passover, make sure the chips are kosher for Passover.

> *¹/₂ cup sugar*
> *pinch of cream of tarter*
> *2 egg whites, beaten until stiff*
> *6 ounces mini chocolate chips*

Fold sugar and tarter into beaten whites. Fold in chips. Drop on foil-lined sheets. Bake at 250 degrees 45–60 minutes or until they feel dry.

SAVORY SPINACH NOODLE PUDDING

Serves 12

This is a good dish to make if someone is already bringing a traditional kugel to a Break the Fast.

> *3 leeks, white part only, sliced*
> *³/₄ cup melted butter or margarine*
> *1 pound broad noodles, barely cooked*
> *6 eggs, lightly beaten*
> *4 packages chopped spinach, thawed and drained*
> *2 cups sour cream (low-fat is okay)*
> *salt and pepper to taste*
> *¹/₂ teaspoon dried thyme*

Sauté leeks in a little butter or margarine until slightly brown. Add to cooked noodles. Add remaining ingredients. Put into buttered baking dish. Place the pan inside another pan filled halfway with water. Bake at 350 degrees for 45 minutes. This recipe may be halved.

APPLESAUCE

Yield 10 servings

For dipping latkes in during Hanukkah.

> *1 quart apple cider*
> *1 tablespoon mulling spice tied in rinsed cheesecloth*
> *5 pounds apples (Granny Smith, Winesap, Macoon, or Delicious; a*
>   *combination of a few kinds is best.)*

Boil apple cider with spices in a large pot until reduced by half. Peel, core, and halve apples. Remove spice bundle and add apples to pot. Cook over medium heat, covered, until apples begin to soften (time depends on type of apple). Remove cover and continue cooking, stirring occasionally, until apples are fully cooked. Mash or leave lumpy. Applesauce may be frozen.

A Jewish guy goes into a deli and points to the display counter and says, "I'll have a pound of that salmon."

"That's not salmon," the clerk says. "That's ham."

The customer says, "In case no one ever told you, you've got a big mouth!"

SALMON CAKES WITH MUSTARD

Makes 8 cakes

Another good dish for Passover.

> *1 pound cooked salmon, skinned and boned, broken into small pieces*
> *2 cups chopped, seeded tomatoes*
> *3 eggs*
> *¹/₂ cup chopped Italian parsley*
> *¹/₂ cup minced shallots*
> *2 tablespoons Dijon mustard*
> *1 tablespoon sieved dry mustard*
> *Salt and pepper to taste*
> *3 cups matzah meal*
> *¹/₂ cup vegetable oil*

Mix salmon, tomatoes, eggs, parsley, shallots, Dijon mustard, sieved dry mustard, salt, pepper, and 1 cup of matzah meal. Form into patties. Dust with remaining matzah meal. Pour oil onto baking sheet. Place in a preheated 450-degree oven for a few minutes. Remove and place patties on sheet and bake 5–7 minutes. Flip and continue cooking for 3–5 minutes. Cakes should be crisp and golden.

HAMANTASCHEN
Yield 36

A variation on a traditional recipe for Purim. The cookies are shaped like the villain Haman's three-pointed hat.

FILLING:
$^1/_3$ *cup pitted prunes*
$^1/_3$ *cup raisins*
$^1/_4$ *cup water*
$^1/_4$ *cup pecans*
$^1/_4$ *apple with peel*
2 tablespoons sugar
juice and peel of $^1/_2$ lemon

DOUGH:
$^2/_3$ *cup butter or margarine*
$^1/_2$ *cup sugar*
1 egg
1 teaspoon vanilla
1 $^1/_2$ –3 cups flour
1 teaspoon baking powder
pinch of salt if using butter

Filling: Simmer prunes and raisins in water, covered, for 15 minutes or until prunes are softened but still firm. Chop in food processor with nuts, apple, and sugar. Add lemon juice and peel.

Dough: Cream butter or margarine and sugar. Add egg and vanilla. Add dry ingredients and mix until smooth. Chill 3 hours or overnight. Divide dough into quarters and roll onto floured surface about $^1/_8$ inch thick. Cut into $2^1/_2$-inch wide circles. Put 1 teaspoon of filling into the center of each circle. With your finger, brush water around the rim of the circle of dough, then press 3 ends together. Top of cookie should be open so that people can see what kind of filling is inside. Bake on greased cookie sheet 10–15 minutes at 375 degrees.

RUGELACH
Yield 3 dozen

A delicious cookie good anytime, except Passover.

DOUGH
$^1/_2$ *pound sweet butter, softened*
$^1/_2$ *pound cream cheese, softened*
2 egg yolks
8 tablespoons sugar
2 teaspoons vanilla
pinch of salt
2 cups flour

FRUIT FILLING
apricot or raspberry preserves
chopped nuts
cinnamon sugar
mini chocolate chips

Cream first 6 dough ingredients. Add flour. Form into ball. Divide into 4 parts and chill if necessary. Roll each part into a circle, spread with fruit filling or chocolate chips then cut into wedges. Starting at the wide end, roll into horns or form into long logs and cut. Bake on ungreased cookie sheets for 25 minutes at 250 degrees.

Chapter 5

From First Kiss to Under the Chuppah: Love and Marriage

I am my beloved's and my beloved is mine.

—Song of Songs 6:3

Every Jewish parent dreams of their son becoming a doctor and their daughter marrying one. But as Mick Jagger* says, you can't always get what you want. Sometimes the daughter grows up to be the doctor. Sometimes the doctor isn't Jewish. And sometimes neither come into the equation.

Whatever the mathematics are, the two of you love each other and want to get married. That's the easy part. Now for the hard part: Jewish parents, even if they're not very religious, have the notion that their children will marry fellow Jews, just as they did. Just as their parents did. And their grandparents and great-grandparents did. And although they may adore you, they may feel compelled to bestow a little guilt. They wouldn't feel like good Jews if they didn't. In fact, at this very moment, they probably are feeling guilty for not raising their son right.

T.G.I.F.

Wouldn't your date be surprised if you whispered in his or her ear after a Friday night date, "It's a mitzvah to *shtup* on Shabbat." A mitzvah is a good deed, and a shtup is . . . well, let's just say you'll have a good time.

. . . .

---

*Mick Jagger of the Rolling Stones, an example of a goy with chutzpah (not to mention one hell of a tuchis).

THE OFFICIAL JEWISH ATTITUDE ON SEX

✡ Sex is a normal, necessary part of life. (Let out a big sigh of relief!)

✡ It is a mitzvah to be fruitful and multiply.

✡ Avoid the extremes. Judaism frowns upon abstinence and overindulgence alike.

✡ The act of sex itself, regardless of procreation, is a vital and integral part of marriage.

COURTSHIP

The epitome of New York Jewishness for this generation is Jerry Seinfeld. Here we have this nice Jewish boy from a good family, and although he's very successful, his job as a comedian is unacceptable to his parents. And who did he used to date? Elaine, a non-Jew from Baltimore, of all places. So why would Jerry throw away centuries of Jewish marriages to go out with Elaine? Because, as his friend George Costanza says, she "has shiksa appeal. Men love the idea of bringing home someone who's not like their mother."

Now you know why you and your significant other get along so well.

Dating someone outside your faith is always an experience. Leah Singer had just started dating Patrick Flynn when, as an ice breaker on their first date, he blurted out, "So, what's it like to be Jewish?"

Avi Gesser had a similar eye-opener: "I was dating a woman while attending university in England. We had been seeing each other for about a month and getting along great, but the sexual aspect of our relationship was stuck at kissing. I was curious as to whether there was a reason for this. I asked, 'Just so I have some idea, how long do you generally need to know someone before you sleep with him?' She responded with the worst possible answer a liberal Jewish boy could hear: 'I cannot have sex with you until I love you as much as Christ.' That was the last time I ever saw her."

As you date, you may go to temple a few times, eat a Passover dinner, or exchange Hanukkah presents. This chapter, along with the holiday chapter, will help with protocol and teach you how not to sound like a *schmuck*. You'll also want to observe your beloved's family traditions and find out how they were passed down. Before you know it, you may be making some traditions of your own.

GETTING HITCHED

Marriage is one of the most basic mitzvahs in Judaism. Therefore, once your partner's parents realize that you are indeed the one for their child, they could be your biggest allies in hastening the wedding. Or maybe it's not the mitzvah but their desire for grandchildren. Regardless, marriage is part of a Jew's religious duty. Man is said to find completion in marriage. Until he is married, he is considered to be only half a man, without joy, peace, or goodness.

Marriage is so important to Jewish life that throughout history unmarried men used to hire a *shadchen*, a matchmaker. While today's shadchen is found in the form of dating services, it was once the domain of a member of the community, usually a middle-aged woman. Shadchens still exist in Israel and Orthodox communities.

Although marriages were often crafted, they were not arranged in the classic sense. Both the man and woman had to agree to it. The Talmud says, "A father is forbidden to marry off his daughter while she is a minor. He must wait until she is grown up and says, 'I want so-and-so.'"* The Talmud looks after the man as well: "A man is forbidden to marry a woman until he first sees her, lest he later find her objectionable and she becomes repulsive to him."** Along the same lines, the *Sefer Hasidim* says, "A youth need not obey his parents if they urge him to marry not the girl he wants, but another with money, for they are not acting properly."***

CHUPPAHS, CAKES, AND CHAIR-DANCING

He popped the question, gave you a ring to die for, and you both are walking around with silly smiles on your faces. Or, after much discussion and soul searching, you agreed to finally tie the knot. Whatever. Now it's time to plan the big day.

You've probably realized by now that the big church wedding is not going to happen. It might not be a temple wedding either. If you're like most couples, you'll incorporate some Jewish rituals as well as some traditions from your heritage into your ceremony. Here's everything you need to know to plan a Jewish wedding. Take from it what you will.

---

*Babylonian Talmud, *Kiddushin* 41a
**Ibid.
****Sefer Hasidim*, paragraph 953.

Marrying off a daughter is like loading cargo onto a ship.

—JEWISH PROVERB

THINGS UNIQUE TO JEWISH WEDDINGS

Ketubah (marriage contract)

Chuppah (wedding canopy)

Procession

Seven blessings

Circling the groom

Yichud (seclusion)

No head table

No announcing the bride and groom

No gift table

Sweet table

Dancing the hora

MIXING IT UP

Really personalize your day by incorporating your multicultural backgrounds into your ceremony. Be creative: Ian and Julie had his uncle play "Hava Negillah" on the bagpipes as a salute to both their heritages. Barry and Lily brought in Chinese dumplings—no pork, though—from her family's favorite restaurant.

Back in biblical times, there were two easy ways to become legally married. *Method #1*: Both partners agree to marry each other. The man gives the woman an item: money, something valuable, or a written commitment to marry her. The woman accepts it. Voilà! They're married. *Method #2*: The couple has sex. Yes, sir, the one-step route to marriage. So, now that you realize you are already married, maybe you won't be so nervous about planning the wedding.

Today, these two methods are combined. The ring represents the valuable item. The ketubah is a contract, and yihud (being alone together after the ceremony) represents consummation. But a lot happens in between.

KETUBAH

The ketubah, or marriage contract, is a legal document stipulating the fundamental conditions that Jewish law place upon a couple before marrying. It is beautifully illustrated and many people frame it. It's a big honor to be one of the two witnesses asked to sign the ketubah. The rabbi reads it aloud in a small ceremony with the bride, groom, witnesses, and maybe a few family members before the wedding. To some, this is the most important part of the wedding day. By Jewish law, once the ketubah is signed, the couple is officially married.

First, you'll need to find a rabbi to marry you and your betrothed. Although traditionally rabbis refuse to perform interfaith marriage ceremonies, nowadays many Reform rabbis will.

Melissa ran into these issues when searching for a rabbi: "When I got married the first time, I wanted to be married by a rabbi. At that time in New York City, there were only a handful of rabbis (all super Reform) who would marry a Jew to a non-Jew, and of those, many had weird little restrictions. Some would marry a Jewish woman to a non-Jewish man but not the other way around. Others would do it in the rabbi's study but not in the sanctuary. Still others would do it but you couldn't get a real ketubah, so it was just a civil ceremony performed by a rabbi. It was all a little alienating, and the second time around, I just went to a judge."

Why won't some rabbis do interfaith ceremonies? Some rabbis feel they cannot ask a non-Jew to commit to all the elements of a Jewish marriage: keeping a Jewish home, raising Jewish children, joining a synagogue, giving to charity, and working for worthy causes. Nor do they wish for a person to make commitments contrary to their own religious beliefs. Also, rabbis who perform interfaith marriages are not allowed to sit on many boards of rabbis, which are made up of local or regional rabbis from different sects of Judaism.

Another word about keeping a Jewish home: As you plan a life together, someone will ask if you will be keeping a Jewish home. This entails observing the Sabbath and celebrating the various festivals and holidays, many of which revolve around the home. Technically, it means keeping a kosher kitchen as well. Today, however, many Jews feel they can keep a Jewish home without keeping kosher. The home always has and will be the Jewish woman's domain. Therefore, it is the woman's responsibility to keep a Jewish

A SPECIAL CHUPPAH

In ancient Israel, the custom was to plant a cedar tree after the birth of a son and a pine or cypress after the birth of a daughter. Chuppah poles used to be made with branches from the trees planted when the bride and groom were born.

. . . .

WEDDING VOCABULARY

Chuppah: the wedding canopy

Hatunah: the Hebrew word for wedding

Kallah: the Hebrew word for bride

Ketubah: the marriage contract

Mazel tov: congratulations.

Machetunim (pronounced "makh-eh-tu-nim"): the relationship that parents of the bride and groom have together after the marriage. They are more than just in-laws. They now have a close bond. They share a common interest in each other's children.

Mezinek (pronounced "meh-zihn-ek"): the youngest male in the family. This term is used at his wedding. It is a great joy for parents to live long enough to see their youngest child married.

Yichud: the fifteen minutes of postceremony seclusion when a couple consummates the marriage.

SIMCHA

Simcha is the Hebrew word for joy. A wedding is a huge simcha.

. . . .

AUFRUF

Note: If your fiancé doesn't know Hebrew or isn't very religious, this next part doesn't apply.

The *aufruf* (pronounced "oof-roof") is the custom of calling the groom up to read from the Torah in synagogue the Saturday morning before his wedding. The rabbi extends his good wishes to the groom and his family during the service. Since there is a custom of the bride and groom not seeing each other for at least a day prior to the wedding, Orthodox brides usually do not attend the aufruf. A bride in the Conservative or Reform movements usually attends with her family. Afterward there is the requisite, post-Jewish-event festive family meal.

home. Keep this in mind. Many non-Jewish women agree to keep a Jewish home to appease their Jewish husbands without realizing that even though the husband wants the Jewish home, it is the wife who will end up doing all of the work.

See if the rabbi at your intended's temple is willing or ask friends for referrals. When you find one, work with your rabbi to design your own ceremony. You can stick to Jewish traditions or incorporate some of the rituals of your own religion; the latter may appease your family, which is always a good thing. And since the wedding party and guest list will most likely include a smattering of other religions, it is always appreciated when the rabbi explains the rituals as he or she goes along, as we will now:

TIMING

Jews don't get married on Shabbat (from sunset Friday to sunset Saturday). This is definitely something to work around. Jews also avoid getting married on Mondays and Wednesdays. In the Middle Ages, people thought these days were unlucky. Now they are just inconvenient.

LOCATION

The ceremony can take place almost anywhere as long as it's under a chuppah, the white silk or satin canopy that people remember most about Jewish weddings. Sometimes chuppahs are made by family members and friends. They can be very elaborate or very simple. Some have biblical quotations embroidered on them. A tallis (prayer shawl) or heirloom tablecloth can also be used as a chuppah. Your caterer or florist may have one as well. The bride and groom stand under the chuppah and recite their vows. Four male relatives or groomsmen hold it aloft on poles.

The chuppah gives the ceremony an air of royalty. And rightly so, as the bride and groom are considered the king and queen of the day. (Just don't let it go to your head or the maid of honor or best man will bring you back down to earth in a hurry.) The chuppah symbolizes the home that the new couple will build together. The bride and groom stand side by side as they will in their new home. The open sides connote that friends and family are always welcome in the home.

The chuppah represents the ancient wedding chamber, which the bridal couple entered for seven days to consummate the wedding. In our fast-paced world, couples get just fifteen minutes to consummate a marriage (see yichud), but you've had quickies before.

The Procession

Everyone's got to get into the act. The immediate family on both sides walks down the aisle. Starting with the groom's family, the order is grandparents, siblings, then both parents flank the groom as he walks down the aisle. Then the bride's family goes in the same order. When the bride and her parents arrive at the altar, the groom lifts the bride's veil, or *bedeken* (pronounced "beh-day-ken"), to make sure she's not somebody else, not wanting to repeat Jacob's biblical mistake. The modest tradition of wearing a veil dates back to when Rebecca covered her face upon seeing Isaac, her betrothed, approaching across the fields.

The Ceremony

At some ceremonies, the bride (and sometimes her parents) circles the groom seven times while holding a lighted candle. This may derive from a cabalistic practice of making a mystic circle to shut out the dastardly demons that resent happiness.

Rather than the bride circling the groom seven times, some modern couples alter the tradition. For example, the bride circles the groom three or four times and then the groom circles the bride three or four times bringing it to a total of seven.

Pretty much at the get-go, the rabbi says the blessing over wine and bread. The bride and groom eat a piece of bread, preferably challah, and sip wine from the same cup. *Tip*: Some brides swear by using white wine—it will do a lot less damage than red if it spills on your precious dress.

Then the bride and groom exchange rings. The ring is a symbol of perfection and unity, a circle without beginning or end. Traditionally, it is simple and unadorned, but nowadays anything goes. The bride and groom exchange rings and vow, "By means of this ring, you are sanctified to me, according to the Law of Moses and Israel."

BOTTOMS UP!

Two cups of wine are shared during the ceremony: one during the Kiddushin and the other during the seven blessings. Some see the first cup as the cup of shared joy and the second as the cup of mutual sacrifice, as the couple will both rejoice and sacrifice together.

CIRCLING THE GROOM

Laura Greenberg and Joe Stewart decided to do the egalitarian version. At the rehearsal, the rabbi explained the tradition but the couple didn't actually practice it. When it came time to do it at the wedding, Joe forgot that Laura was supposed to go first. They both started circling each other at the same time and ended up doing an awkward "do-si-do" instead.

ONE IS ALL YOU NEED

Around C.E. 1000, Jewish law officially outlawed polygamy. In biblical times, when they were trying to populate a nation, it was useful. But then it sort of lost its appeal. Plus, the Torah doesn't make it sound so great. Remember all the trouble between Jacob and his four wives? Polygamy dropped out of general practice long before it was against the law. Maybe the Israelites realized that it was too hard a bed to lie in. For example, none of the two thousand rabbis cited in the Talmud had multiple wives.

The rabbi blesses the couple with the Sheva Berachot, or seven blessings. The blessings praise God for creating man and woman, express hope that the bride and groom will be happy together, and sanctify the bride and groom's commitment to each other.

BREAKING THE GLASS

The rabbi says the benediction over one glass, and the bride and groom sip from another. The shared cup of wine is a reminder of the bride and groom's common destiny. From now on their lives will be inseparable.

Then the groom steps on a glass, usually a delicate wine or champagne glass wrapped in a napkin (although some use lightbulbs that are easier to crush). Occasionally the bride and the groom both stomp on the glass. Before you demonstrate your equality, check the quality of your shoe's sole. Most dainty wedding shoes are not made for stomping on anything, let alone glass. With the crushing of the glass, however it happens, the wedding guests cheer wildly.

WHY ALL OF THIS DESTRUCTION OF PERFECTLY GOOD STEMWARE?

There are several interpretations:
- ✡ To symbolize the destruction of the ancient Temple
- ✡ To remember the suffering of others even during the happiest celebrations
- ✡ To remind us of life's fragility and that happiness is transient

Yes, it's a lot heavier than you might have expected, what with all the clapping and cheering. Judaism always comes back to suffering, enslavement, and persecution, but never fear, the mood is alleviated by a good meal.

As the bride and groom lead the processional away from the chuppah, the guests clap in time with the music. The couple goes directly to a quiet room to spend about fifteen minutes alone together. This tradition, called the yichud (pronounced "yih-who'd") dates back to ancient times when the groom and his bride would consummate the marriage. If you think your fiancé's family is meddlesome, they're nothing compared to their ancestors. In the good old days, family members and wedding guests would wait outside the door of the yichud until the groom emerged with a bloodstained sheet, proving that the marriage had been consummated—and presumably that the bride was a virgin!

These days, it's unlikely that the bride and groom haven't already slept together. It's also unlikely that they're going to get it on just steps away from the wedding guests. Instead, couples take this time to enjoy at least part of their big day in private and maybe grab a bite to eat. After a few minutes of quiet respite, the bride and groom emerge to celebrate as husband and wife.

THE RECEPTION

You don't have to hire a kosher caterer. However, you may consider having a fish or vegetarian alternative dish for the rabbi and relatives who keep kosher. And your trendy vegan friends will thank you, too.

Singing and dancing is a crucial part of the Jewish wedding, and we don't just mean "Celebration" and the "Electric Slide." With the first few notes of "Hava Negillah," the party really starts rocking. Elderly relatives, shy cousins, and usually reserved adults clamor onto the floor to dance the hora.

Inevitably, someone will grab chairs for the newlyweds, and you will be asked to sit in them. Be sure to hold on tight when the larger members of the party raise the chairs. What happens next is a bit like stage diving into a crowd. The two of you will bob along above everyone, peering down at bald spots and towering bridesmaid up-dos. You will hold the corners of a tallis or handkerchief so you will always be connected while dancing—and through life. *Tip*: Before the ceremony, remind the men to lean the chair slightly backward—many a bride and groom have slipped off and onto the floor. Or just hope that there is a nice Jewish chiropractor on the guest list.

AS IF WEDDING DAYS WEREN'T HARD ENOUGH

Under the old laws, the bride and groom fasted on their wedding day to atone for past sins and start married life with a clean slate. In the synagogue, the groom would recite the Yom Kippur (Day of Atonement) confession before the congregation.

TIP

Don't bring a present to a Jewish wedding; there is no gift table. On the other hand, cash is always accepted. Gifts should be sent or brought to the couple's home.

HAT HEAD

Alan Foppiano was excited to go to his first Jewish wedding. He was delighted when someone handed him a yarmulke on his way into the synagogue. He put the skullcap on his head and immediately forgot about it. Hours later, toward the end of the reception, the bride's brother approached Alan saying, "You can always tell who the non-Jews are. They never want to take the yarmulke off."

(*Note*: Some Jews always wear a yarmulke. Reform Jews usually only wear them when in the synagogue.)

How to Dance the Hora

Participants form a large circle and hold hands. Take a step to the right with your right foot. Then step with your left foot across in front of your right. Step to the right again with your right foot. Bring your left foot across behind your right and step right with your right foot. Repeat.

Beware that periodically, usually on a whim, someone will decide to change directions and inevitably everyone will crash into each other. Also, every so often the group will raise their arms and run into the center of the circle and back out again. Or a leader might break off and snake the dancers around the room, something like a conga line. At some point, the bride and groom will be lifted onto chairs in the center.

The beauty of the hora is that it is organized chaos. Don't worry about stepping out of turn. This ain't no line dance.

Fun Facts and Lore

✡ The Talmud set eighteen as the proper age for marriage.

✡ According to legend, forty days before a child is born, its bride or groom is determined in heaven.

✡ It was customary for teachers to adjourn their classes and join a wedding party with their students: It was a mitzvah to participate in the happiness of the bride and groom.

✡ Most shtetl weddings occurred on Fridays, in order to give everyone a chance to celebrate on the Sabbath.

✡ Upon marriage, all past sins are forgiven.

Orthodox Wedding Traditions

✡ The bride and groom do not see each other for at least one day prior to getting married.

✡ Orthodoxy uses all three methods of getting married: ring, contract, and yichud. Newlyweds actually leave the reception to have sex. It's part of the ritual.

✡ The wedding celebration lasts for seven days. This traces back to the Bible's account of the festivities after Jacob married Leah. In those days, each wedding added to Israel's estate and population growth.

Everybody in the Pool!

The *mikvah,* or ritual bath, is part of the Orthodox tradition. The men go to the mikvah on Friday afternoons to clean themselves for the Sabbath. The women go monthly after their periods to purify themselves before having sex with their husbands, which is considered a holy act. (Now you know why some Jewish guys think they are God's gift to women.) It is more common among the different sects of Judaism for a woman to go to the mikvah just before getting married. The ritual bathing is a bit of an ordeal, but if it makes sex holy, who can argue?

Not Getting Enough?

Underserved wives might want to tell their husbands about *onah,* the wife's conjugal rights. According to Jewish law, marital relations are the privilege of the wife and the duty of the husband.

Women were considered more inhibited than men when it came to expressing their sexual desires. Therefore, the man is obligated to initiate sex when he thinks his wife wants it. But, he can never force himself on her. To ensure that Jewish wives were sexually fulfilled, the rabbis prescribed the following sexual schedule* arranged according to the husband's profession. How often are you supposed to shtup (make love)? See below:

WHO	WHEN
Men of independent means	Every day
Laborers	Twice a week
Donkey drivers	Once a week
Camel drivers	Once a month
Sailors	Once every six months

*Mishna Ketubot 5:6

WHAT IS KLEZMER MUSIC AND WHY DO I HAVE TO LISTEN TO IT AT MY WEDDING?

Klezmer music is the instrumental music heard at Jewish functions. It has a very old traditional Eastern European sound—that's where it comes from—and many feel it should have stayed there. However, others don't, and since it is a part of the culture, you usually have at least a smattering of it at a Jewish wedding.

IS ANY PLACE SETTING SAFE?

Glasses and guests are not the only things to get smashed at a Jewish wedding. Plate breaking is a vestigial practice from the days of arranged marriages. The mothers of the bride and groom smash a piece of crockery to represent a breaking of the mother-child ties and in recognition of the new tie between husband and wife.

SWEET TABLE

This dessert table is piled with cakes, cookies, and chocolates and guaranteed to break the will of the most disciplined dieter. Many argue that this is the high point of any large Jewish celebration. In fact, after attending her first Jewish wedding, the very Catholic Christina Egan exclaimed, "I want to be Jewish so I can have my wedding at the Standard Club,* dance the hora, and have a sweet table!"

------

*Very expensive, exclusive, predominantly Jewish club in Chicago.

. . . .

WHEN "SHALOM" MEANS GOOD-BYE

Judaism makes allowances for divorce. While it is not encouraged, the religion realizes that certain marriages just don't work and should be terminated. There are, however, specific steps to ending a marriage. First, there must be mediation. This thankless job usually falls upon the rabbi, who initially prescribes a cooling off period for the couple. Next, he insists that they attempt to reconcile. If this is not successful, the husband gives his wife a bill of divorcement, which is called the *get*. Once a get is got, the marriage is over. A civil divorce is not enough. A couple must go through this process to be separated in the eyes of God.

> "
> *Why do Jewish divorces cost so much? They're worth it.*
> *Why do Jewish guys die before their wives? They want to.*"
>
> —HENNY YOUNGMAN

Chapter 6

Family Matters,
It *Really* Matters

The *Jew/non-Jew issue* probably comes up most when dealing with families. You are on your own trying to convince your family that this Jewish man or woman is the ideal partner for you. We can, however, help you feel a little more comfortable around the family.

A Jewish family can be overwhelming. They can be noisy, emotional, quick to anger, and even quicker to kiss and make up. Jews love drama. Everything is a very big deal. If you yourself come from a reserved family, this could take a little getting used to. Start now, because family is a high priority for Jews. God knows family occasions are a big deal. And don't let anyone tell you differently—when you marry a Jew, you marry the whole family.

Mishpocheh (pronounced "mish-puh-keh") means family in Yiddish. If you hear someone saying "They're mishpocheh!" despite how it sounds, what they are actually saying is that this person can do no wrong or at least will be forgiven anything because they are family. While Jews have always been very connected to their community, the family unit takes precedence over everything.

If you haven't met the family yet, here's a quick prep guide. Remember, the tougher they are on you, the more they like you.

JEWISH STANDARD TIME

Every Jewish function starts at least fifteen minutes late. If you're making reservations for your sweetheart's family, be sure to allow time for finding the perfect parking space, gabbing with friends they meet on the street, ducking into a boutique to see what's on sale, and so on. Sometimes the reason for being late is more interesting than the event they were late to.

. . . .

1. Stuff yourself the entire week before the visit. Your stomach must be expanded in order to accommodate the massive quantities of food that will be forced upon you by the mother. Girls, if you object to the feeding, you will from that moment on be known as "my son's girlfriend, the anorectic."

2. Get ready to be cornered. Jewish families think they are just making conversation, but those with less intrusive families might feel invaded.

3. If you come from a mild-mannered, reserved family, prepare yourself before meeting your partner's family. Jews talk with their mouths *and* their hands. Meal times turn into forums for just about everything, from the sister's hairstyle to the neighbors' gall for buying such an expensive car to a cousin's new position in the family business. No one is safe. If you don't think your delicate voice will be heard, turn the TV on really loud and practice yelling over it. Rock concerts, crowded bars, and bowling alleys are also good places to prep your vocal cords for meeting the family.

4. Learn how to answer every question with another question. Some might find this argumentative but we look at it as being analytical. It's good practice for lawyers in training.

Jew #1: "What would you like for your birthday?"
Jew #2: "What would I like for my birthday? What do you mean what would I like for my birthday? Who says you have to get me a birthday present?"

5. You might want to bring a little gift when visiting the family. There is an old Hebrew proverb that says "A guest who comes empty-handed does not deserve a warm welcome." Flowers are always nice.

6. If your Jewish in-laws invite you somewhere, regard it as a summons. There is no such thing as politely declining. You're going whether you want to or not.

Since most Jewish social gatherings revolve around food, the first time you meet the family will most likely be at a meal. Whether it's a holiday meal or lunch at a deli, you're bound to come across some foreign foods, like chopped liver. Here's how one Jewish girl prepped her boyfriend.

Lisa Goldberg decided to bring Steve home to meet her family. Having dated him for some time, Lisa knew Steve to be a picky and unadventurous eater. She also knew that her mother would serve chopped liver made from a favorite old family recipe. Although Lisa liked chopped liver, she realized that most people do not. To prevent Steve from taking one whiff of her mom's creation and losing his lunch, she decided to condition him. Lisa insists that the method below will prepare even the most weak-stomached WASP for any Jewish culinary atrocities that might come their way:

1. Go to the store and buy some chopped liver.
2. When you get home, bring chopped liver into the bathroom.
3. Open lid and wave container in front of face.
4. Vomit into toilet, as necessary.
5. Repeat until you can see and smell chopped liver without getting nauseous.

This could take awhile. However, you only need to be able to be around it without retching. When it is offered, it is okay to politely decline. As many Jews themselves are disgusted by it, it would be cruel and unusual if you were forced to actually ingest any. Then again, you might want to try it. Some people really like it.

JEWISH PARENTS

You are a wonderful person. Anyone would be lucky to have you. Jewish parents, however, are likely to feel otherwise. Unfortunately, most Jewish parents are not going to welcome a child's relationship with a non-Jew. They might like you as a person. But the sad truth is that they won't want you as a son- or daughter-in-law. It's not you; it's your non-Jewishness. Here are some of their worst nightmares:

SPEAK UP

"Never apologize for sharing feeling. When you do so, you apologize for truth."

—BENJAMIN DISRAELI

1. Their friends pointedly ask "So is this Maria Jewish?" taking a little wind out of the sails on the S.S. *My Son the Doctor Is Getting Married.*

SHOW SOME RESPECT!

Jewish children are not supposed to call their parents by their first names, occupy the father's seat, or contradict him in public.

. . . .

2. Your wedding reception will be held at your parents' country club that has two Jewish members.

3. Their grandchildren are going to turn out to be Jesus freaks.

4. Who is going to buy the candles and remind their son to go to temple on their *yahrtzeit* (death anniversary)?

5. Their son is turning his back on them and their way of life. They are a source of embarrassment to him.

THE TIES THAT BIND

Jewish parents strive to achieve a unique balance. They simultaneously spoil and demand the world of their children. While they try to provide their kids with every material comfort available, Jewish parents expect their kids to excel in school or at their jobs. Slacker Jewish kids do not fare as well as the garden variety. Maybe you're thinking, "That's not true. My boyfriend's a slacker and his parents give him a lot." Well, just imagine the benefits he'd receive if he actually got off his butt and found a real job.

Fortunately for the kids, the parents' perceptions of their children often vary. This variance can usually be attributed to the sex of both the parents and the children. Fathers find fault with their sons and are generally lenient with their daughters. Mothers tend to nitpick their daughters while their sons can do no wrong.

THE JEWISH MOTHER

Realize right off the bat that you are not good enough for her child. No one is. At first you might think it's because you're not Jewish. Later you will realize that it's really because you aren't her.

You'll feel better when you see that it's not just you that's not good enough. Nothing is good enough for the Jewish mother. If you want proof, start going to restaurants with a Jewish mother. Unless you happen to eat at one of her absolute favorite restaurants, everywhere you go will have problems. The service will be too slow, the fish overcooked, or the decor garish. At least you'll know it's not only you.

If your partner's mom does not fit this description, don't doubt the credibility of this book. Consider yourself lucky and read on.

A True Story

A nice Catholic boy named Dave tells of his close encounter with a Jewish mother.

"I'm a reluctant Catholic. I started dating this Jewish girl a few years ago and things were going well. But it was the same old story: boy meets girl; girl goes to live on a kibbutz in Israel.

A year and a half later, I'm in New York on business, staying in a suite at the Plaza. I get a voicemail from the girl saying that she's at her parents' house on Long Island and that she just got in a day earlier from Israel. She wanted to come to Boston (where I lived) to see me.

I called her back and told her that, as luck would have it, I was in New York, and that she should come and stay with me for the week. She agreed.

When she got to the hotel, she repeated the conversation she had with her mother:

Girl: I'm going into the city to see Dave.

Mother: Who's this Dave?

Girl: You know Dave, the guy that I was seeing before I went to Israel.

Mother: Dave what?

Girl: Nolan.

Mother: Oh, so when will you be back?

Girl: Later in the week.

Mother: Where will you be sleeping?

Girl: I suppose at the hotel. We did date for a while.

Mother: My daughter, home for one day, then heading off to spend a week with a boy I've never met. So, where is this Dave staying?

Girl: At the Plaza.

Mother: I have always liked that David!

THE MOTHER/SON RELATIONSHIP

There is no relationship like that of a Jewish mother and her son. In his mother's eyes, the son can do no wrong. To the rest of the family, he might be a no-good bum. To the mother, he is a prince.

Your boyfriend might say he thinks his mother is too pushy, too

STILL LIFE WITH MOTHER

There comes a time in every man's life when he must stand up and tell his mother that he is an adult. This usually happens around age forty-five.

STAYING POWER

QUESTION: *What's the difference between a Jewish mother and a rottweiler?*

ANSWER: *Eventually the rottweiler lets go.*

MOTHERLY LOVE

"Mrs. Rosen," the psychiatrist says, "there is nothing wrong with your son physically. However, he does have an Oedipus complex."

"Oedipus, schmedipus," Mrs. Rosen says. "Just as long as he loves his mother."

involved in his life, and so on. But he'll never do anything about it. Nor should he. He knows that in times of trouble, he can always turn to Mom.

A TIP FROM SOMEONE WHO'S BEEN THERE

"Although I'm black," says Shelley Weaver, "I've dated more than my fair share of Jewish boys. My one and only tip that I have picked up from dating Jewish men is that if their mother doesn't like you, you're screwed. My longest relationship lasted, despite my not being Jewish, for over a year largely because his mother loved me. All the previous non-Jewish girlfriends had been swiftly kicked to the curb."

THE JEWISH MOTHER-IN-LAW

Don't kid yourself by thinking it's going to be easier once you're married. Things are only going to get worse. You think Jewish mothers are a lot to handle? You think mothers-in-law in general are difficult? Try combining the two. It's going to be ten times worse than anything you can imagine.

And this is not because you're not Jewish. Jewish in-laws, brides in particular, are tortured by their mothers-in-law as well. Maybe even more than you will be. This stems from the fact that Jewish women in general are very strong and opinionated. You might be able to look past your mother-in-law's behavior and move on. Pit two Jewish women against each other and watch the fireworks. Once married, you could actually become the favored in-law because you don't give your mother-in-law as much of a headache as that prince or princess her other kid married.

Not only is nothing good enough for the Jewish mother, she feels it's her job to make the world a much better place by pointing out a much better way to do almost everything. Think of it as enthusiasm. If she didn't care so much, she wouldn't bother to say anything. Jewish mothers just like to be involved. Whether it's how you make tuna salad or how you are spending your weekends, the Jewish mother knows that her input is crucial. Just know that nothing is your own business. The day you marry into a Jewish family, say good-bye to your privacy. After all, now you're mishpocheh.

There is also the guilt. Jews feel guilty about everything. A few things play into this guilt complex. First, there is a lot of survivor's guilt. This has been true throughout history. The Holocaust spurred most of the survivor's guilt in the past few generations.

The other thing is a feeling of responsibility. Judaism holds that mankind can save the world through individual acts. Every mitzvah counts. This leads to the feeling of never doing enough. There is always something else you could have done if you only had the time, the energy, or the forethought. Are you feeling guilty yet?

Finally, there are everyday occurrences that can cause you to have a guilty conscience: You forgot your great-aunt Sadie's birthday again. You neglected to pick up a marble rye for the luncheon at your sister-in-law's house. Your guests are late because you forgot to tell them that finding a parking space in your neighborhood is murder.

Don't hesitate to talk about your guilt. You should feel guilty if you don't.

THE JEWISH FATHER

While the mother is in charge of the home, the father is charged with being the breadwinner. In addition to professional careers (law and medicine), Jews gravitate to business. When they first came to the United States, Jews took small-scale service jobs such as tailors, storekeepers, jewelers, and butchers. Striving to give their children a better life, many built successful businesses.

Drive is one of the central traits of the Jewish male. The Jewish grandparents were most likely immigrants who came to America with next to nothing. They struggled to give their kids opportunities they never had. This has been the case for each generation until now. Your mate probably is not driven to do better than his or her parents because, statistically, the chances of doing so are very slim. Still, if you are dating a Jewish guy, he should be highly motivated; it's part of his genetic makeup. If he's not, return him immediately and get a better Jew.

"Adam was the luckiest of men. He had no mother-in-law."

—JEWISH PROVERB

"*I don't know what to do," Barry tells his friend Josh. "My mother hates every girl I bring home."*

"*Here's what you do," Josh says. "Bring home a girl who looks just like your mother. Then she's sure to like her."*

Barry and Josh meet several weeks later. "So," says Josh, "did you take my advice?"

"*Yes," Barry says. "I found a girl who looked just like my mom, same height, same coloring. She even had a similar personality."*

"*And what happened?"*

"*My father couldn't stand her."*

> *A Jewish boy comes home from school and tells his mother he got a part in the school play. The mother thinks this is wonderful and asks what part he will be playing. "I play the role of the Jewish husband."*
>
> *The mother scowls and says, "Go back to your teacher and tell her that you want a speaking part!"*

Most Jewish fathers are very interested in their children's day-to-day activities and will demand a full accounting of their lives at the dinner table. Don't be taken aback if your partner's father constantly interrupts with stories and jokes of his own. Be sure to laugh loudly, which won't be that hard to do since Jews are notoriously great story-tellers. However, be prepared to hear the same stories over and over again in the future. Despite all the jokes and stories, Jewish fathers usually talk less than Jewish mothers, but not much.

The Jewish father is typically pretty hard on his son. After all, the son has a lot to live up to. It is the father's job to make sure that his offspring turn out to be as successful as possible. This is what he

GOOD ADVICE

1. Parents (especially mothers) of Jewish guys never really let go. A thirty-year-old Jewish lawyer I dated still doesn't buy his own suits; he "wouldn't want to offend his mother." The parents of non-Jewish guys are more likely to cut the cord upon college graduation.

2. All Jewish family get-togethers revolve around food, and lots of it. It is the responsibility of the hostess to keep trying to stuff her guests long after they are too stuffed to breathe. Note to non-Jews: Refusing food from the hostess is like slapping her in the face.

3. Jewish families tend to be much more direct with each other. There's no beating around the bush, so there's loads of gratuitous advice (which you'll never hear the end of if you don't follow) going around the table.

4. The women rule the house.

5. Jewish men have little-to-no Tim Allen/home improvement—like skills. This is what independent contractors are for.

6. Jews never waste any food. Any leftovers that can't be forced into an innocent mouth will be scraped back into its original container, no matter how small the remaining scrap.

—ALISON LEVY, NEW YORK CITY

cares about most. Therefore, as long as the son is making a decent living, Dad might not mind if he's with a lovely shiksa. In fact, if you are the said shiksa, Dad might be your biggest ally. Remember, in their innermost being, every Jewish guy wants a shiksa of his own. Not because non-Jewish women are that different from Jewish women, but because they have always been *verboten*. Dad might be proud that his son entered lands where he dared not go.

As the Jewish mother thinks that no one is good enough for her son, the Jewish father is very protective of his daughter. Generally, he regards her as his little princess and expects that other men will treat her accordingly. Unfortunately, many girls grow accustomed to this type of attention, hence the title Jewish American Princess.

Tip: When in doubt, ask questions. First, it shows you are interested. More important, they will think you are intelligent. Jews are encouraged to question everything.

THE GRANDPARENTS

If your beau's parents are having a hard time accepting that their kid is with a goy, chances are it's because they are afraid of how their own parents will react. The grandparents might be the least accepting of the interfaith relationship, which is completely out of their frame of reference. We are the first generation where interfaith dating is the norm. Dating non-Jews was practically unheard of in their time.

In fact, Jews traditionally sat *shivah** for children who married non-Jews. That's right. If their children married non-Jews they were dead to them. No matter how much trouble your boyfriend's family might have with your relationship, if they are still acknowledging his existence, consider yourself ahead of the game. For more on the older generation's perspective on this, you might want to rent the movie *Fiddler on the Roof*.

When the grandparents do warm up to you, they're not shy about it. David from Scarsdale, New York, recalls these precious moments with Grandma: "One day my friend Jane and I decided to stop by my grandmother's house. She has a beautiful home so she

*The Jewish equivalent of a wake; see page 128.

A NOTE ON POLITICS

No matter how wealthy, most Jews are Democrats. After thousands of years of persecution, the Jews traditionally side with the underdog. They tend to vote on social issues more than what would benefit them economically. So you might want to keep your "Rush Limbaugh for President" pin well hidden around his or her folks.

● ● ● ● ● ● ● ● ● ● ● ● ● ● ● ● ● ●

"*Israel is the land of milk and honey; Florida is the land of Milk of Magnesia.*"

"*A little boy returned home from his first day at school. His mother ran to the door to greet him. "So tell me, bubeleh," she said, "how was school?"*

He replied, "It was fine, Mama."

"Did you learn anything, bubeleh?"

"Yes, I learned that my name is Irving!""

gave Jane a tour. In one of the upstairs hallways, they stopped to admire a photo taken at my sister's wedding. And Grandma looks at Jane and says, 'It's been so long since we've had a wedding in the family.' It was kind of embarrassing but really funny since Jane and I weren't romantically involved at all and my grandmother had never even met her before. It was much worse when we went to see a girlfriend of mine when she was in our high school play. Afterward, when we were congratulating her on her performance, Grandma hugged her and said, 'I hope you're one of ours someday.'"

Fortunately, every winter vast numbers of Jewish grandparents migrate to somewhere near or within Miami Beach. Some even live there year-round. Florida (pronounced "Flah-rih-daaah") grandparents are the very best kind. Think of all the free tropical vacations the grandkids get. There is also the peace of mind. If your grandparents are playing bridge at the beach, you don't have to worry about them slipping on the ice in Chicago or getting mugged in New York.

Many Jewish families call their grandparents Bubbe and Zadie (pronounced "zay-dee") rather than Grandma and Grandpa. Children and loved ones are also called *bubeleh*, which is a term of endearment and usually accompanied by an exclamation like "You're good enough to eat!" If you really want to hear some colorful Yiddish, hang out around the grandparents. And you'll be sure to get a good meal out of the deal. Before Bruce and Jenni visited his bubbe, Bruce warned Jenni that his grandmother was a "food pusher." Jenni, a slight woman, had never been a big eater. She decided to train by eating more and more in the days leading up to the visit. At the dinner at Bubbe's, Jenni was pretty impressed with herself. She ate a big first helping and then went on to seconds and even thirds. By the time Bubbe came around offering fourths, Jenni couldn't eat another bite and politely declined. Upon which Bubbe frowned and said, "Don't you like my cooking?"

ZEN AND THE ART OF YIDDISH

We put a lot of Yiddish and Hebrew definitions in this book so that you can understand the funny-sounding words that pepper conversations. But be careful about using it yourself. It's easy to make a mistake. For example, the day finally came when non-Jewish Paul was to meet his Jewish girlfriend Rebecca's dad. Rebecca had told her dad that Paul was Jewish, so she told Paul to just go with the flow. Paul felt comfortable with the Yiddish words he'd picked up from Rebecca, and thought he could pull it off. At lunch, everything was going great, and her father didn't catch on to a thing. Just as Rebecca began to stop worrying, her dad took a big bite of his knish and got a gob of mustard on his cheek. Before she could say anything, Paul blurted out, "You have some schmuck on your face!"*

Laugh now, but one day you'll be driving a big Cadillac and eating dinner at four in the afternoon.

YIDDISH GLOSSARY

Browse through for words you didn't know were Yiddish, ultra-descriptive words for just the right circumstance, and words you may overhear at your loved one's house.

Bubkes (bub-kes): Russian for beans, as in "I worked all this time for what? Bubkes!"

Chutzpah: Guts and gall rolled into one

Cockamamy: ridiculous

Dreck: junk

Farblondjet (far-blon-jet): really, really lost, way off track

Feh: basically saying something stinks, literally and figuratively, as in "Feh! My matzah ball soup is cold."

Gesundheit (geh-sund-height): health; what you say when someone sneezes

Glitch: risky undertaking, or a slip up

Gonif: thief

Kibitz: to comment, to joke, tease; running commentary

Klutz: bungling person

Kvetch: person or verb, complaining, never comfortable

Maven: expert, which every Jew thinks he is on every subject

---

*Did you figure out where Paul made his fatal mistake? Schmutz means dirt but can be used to identify any substance that shouldn't be there whether it's food on the face or crud on a sweater. Schmuck, on the other hand, is the Yiddish term for jerk, but its literal translation describes a certain part of the male anatomy. So, you can imagine what Rebecca's father's reaction was.

Avoid saying anything in German, especially around the grandparents. A legacy from the Holocaust, almost anything German makes most Jews' skin crawl.

• • • • • • • • • • • • • • • • • • • •

Mensch: a good man

Meshuggener: crazy

Mishegoss: madness

Momzer: child of an adulteress or incestuous relationships

Naches: joy; usually children bring this on

Ongepotchket: all done up, usually referring to a woman's over-the-top outfit

Plotz: to explode, usually by being aggravated

Potchkeh: fuss or mess around

Putz: fool, more offensive than schmuck

Schlemiel: foolish person, clumsy; made famous by "Laverne and Shirley" theme song

Schlep, schlepper: to drag, or someone who isn't a good worker

Schlimazel: born loser

Schlock: cheap

Schmuck: the male anatomy; a jerk

Schmo: like any old Joe but usually the butt of a joke

Schmooz: chitchat

Shlump: to drag around, shuffle, or a drip, a slovenly person

Shmatte: rag, as in "I love your dress." "Oh, this old shmatte?"

Shmegegge (shma-geg-gee): a drip

Shmendrick: weak, thin person

Shnoz, shnozzola: large nose

Shtick: short comedy material

Shvitz: to sweat

Yenta: a gossip

A True Story

Joseph Gold recalls bringing his non-Jewish girlfriend home to his parents' house for dinner back in the sixties. Joseph's grandparents were living with the family, and so was Yiddish. Rather than tell his parents that his girlfriend was a shiksa, he tried to pass her off as a Jew. He explained her speechlessness by feigning incredulousness and saying, "In Jody's house, they don't speak Yiddish."

Now that you have the meanings down, here's a suggestion from Jeffrey Rotblatt on how to get your mouth to say the tricky Yiddish sounds.

"About a dozen years ago, I was dating a gentile woman who worked for a Hollywood lawyer. She knew he was a *macher* who liked to putz around the office. She could tell me about his schmoozing and carry on about the schlemiels they had to work with. But try as she might, she couldn't properly express frustration with his whining. She came close, "kah-vetch," "kuh-vetch," and "keh-vetch" were all strong attempts, but, alas, remained multisyllabic.

"Fortunately, she was dating me. I had her try the following exercises:

1. Say "ketchup"
2. Say "vegetable"
3. Repeat steps 1 and 2 rapidly, as in "ketchup-vegetable" followed by "vegetable-ketchup"
4. Take a deep breath
5. Now, without pausing to think about it, try to say both words at once. If you don't let your brain get in the way, the only plausible result is "kvetchtable," from which it's an easy step to "kvetch."

"After a decade not only can she still say kvetch, but she teaches others how to say it."

A TIP FOR YOUR FAMILY

Liz was the first Jew her future mother-in-law had ever met. Shortly before the wedding, Liz and her fiancé Peter asked their moms to go out to lunch together to get to know each other. Having such different backgrounds, conversation did not flow easily. So, presumably to break the ice, Peter's mom decided to tell a joke: "A priest and a rabbi were in a boat together. . . ."

BIDDING ADIEU

"Wasps leave and never say good-bye. Jews say good-bye and never leave."

Chapter 7

We've All Got to Go Sometime: Funeral Traditions

"Death is more universal than life; everyone dies but not everyone lives."

—A. SACHS

"L'CHAIM!"

Why toast *"to life"* at the beginning of a chapter about death? Because Judaism places all emphasis on life on Earth, and not the afterlife and heaven. Dying is not popular. In fact, death is rarely even discussed in Jewish writings. Unlike most religions, the afterlife is really just an afterthought for Jews. Death comes to everyone but is devoid of any virtue. The focus of Judaism is on leading a good life on Earth.

Unfortunately, there isn't a consensus in the Jewish community on the hereafter issue. Since the Torah doesn't mention the afterlife, Jews don't think about it much. Between Torah study and trying to uphold 613 commandments, who has time? Possible reasons for the Torah not mentioning the afterlife are:

✡ The Israelites were basically sick of the issue. The Torah was written right after they were slaves in Egypt, where the afterlife was an obsession and many slaves were worked to death building the pyramids and giant tombs.

✡ It could divert Jews' attention from their responsibilities in this life.

Yet Jews do believe in the concept of Gan Eden,* or Paradise. When a person dies, survivors pray that his soul rests in Gan Eden. There is a place for every Jewish soul. Anyone—even a non-Jew—who is righteous has a place in Paradise. If you do good, you get to go to Heaven. Not a bad deal.

Just as there are prayers for Heaven, there are also Hebrew and Yiddish curses wishing people to Hell. Confused yet? There isn't much talk about Heaven and Hell, since the big emphasis is on life. Why worry about it when there are plenty of other things to lose sleep over: Whether you are going to do Passover or have to schlep over to your sister's, how much it's going to cost to fix the dishwasher or if it really is just water weight . . . these are things to worry about!

In the World-to-Come, there will be no eating or drinking or procreation or business or jealousy or hatred or competition, but the righteous will sit with crowns on their heads feasting on the radiance of the shekhina, the divine presence.

—BABYLONIAN TALMUD, *BERAKHOT* 17a

JEWISH VIEW ON SATAN

While not a major player, Satan does exist according to Jewish liturgy. He tempts man to sin but is not entirely evil, as he is one of God's angels.

JEWISH VIEW ON ANGELS

Angels are God's helpers. They are supernatural. While they may sometimes take the shape of man, they were never mortal. Dead people do go to Heaven but they don't become angels.

BEFORE THE FUNERAL

A dead body cannot be left unattended. Anyone can watch over the deceased for the night. It doesn't have to be a relative. And it couldn't hurt to have this person be an observant Jew who would read from the book of psalms while on post.

---

*Gan Eden, which translates to Garden of Eden, also refers to the biblical garden God planted and into which Adam was placed.

If a person is near death, it is forbidden to leave him, so that he should not die alone.

—SHULKHAN ARUKH, YOREH DE'AH 339:4

THE END-ALL BE-ALL: THE ORTHODOX VIEW ON DEATH

According to the Orthodoxy, the soul can undergo divine judgment for up to a year. The good get to zoom straight up to Gan Eden.

In Heaven, there is no eating, drinking, or sex. The righteous sit and enjoy the rays of God. Shabbat is supposed to give us a glimpse of Paradise. However, Paradise is supposed to be about a trillion times more joyous and blissful. According to the Talmud, only a handful of souls in history have not gone to Paradise. These are truly evil people, and their souls disintegrate and disappear.

DRESS REHEARSAL

Though few actually do it, every year on Yom Kippur, Jews are supposed to wear the *kittel,* a plain white linen garment. While the kittel symbolizes status and freedom, it is also the clothing in which Jews are to be buried. Wearing one's death garments makes a person realize that his days on Earth are numbered and passing quickly. It really drives the point home that if there is an argument to settle, a fence to mend, or a hand to hold, today is the day to do it. Before it is too late.

The closest most Jews come to believing in an afterlife is saying that when a person dies, they live on through other people's memory of them. So you don't want to screw up and have people curse you after you're gone. Therefore, from a very young age, Jews are taught that it's important to make contributions to society during their lifetime.

This might help explain why many Jews are considered overachievers. Jews believe that humanity's goal is to essentially fix the world and bring peace to all. In fact, psychoanalysis, chemotherapy, and the polio vaccine were developed by Jews.

You're also obligated to enjoy life while you're living it. It says in the Scriptures, "Thou shalt rejoice before the Lord, thy God." So, now you have permission to go forth and celebrate the joys of the body—such as food, drink, and merriment—as well as those of the spirit—charity, worship, and study.

THE COMING OF THE MESSIAH

While Christians believe that Jesus Christ was the Messiah, the Jews are still waiting for the Messiah. A descendant of the house of David will redeem humanity and establish the reign of God on Earth. Instead of a cherubic angel coming down from Heaven, Elijah the Prophet is the one who heralds the Messiah. During Passover, Jews leave the front door open and set out an extra glass of wine just in case he decides to drop in.

Most Jews today think of the Messiah as humanity collectively. It is believed that humanity can usher in the realm of God by its own actions of kindness, justness, and enlightenment. This also contributes to why the Jews place so much emphasis on kindness and doing good deeds.

Although it is rarely, if ever, mentioned in the Reform movement, according to Judaism, we are more than matter. More than flesh and blood. Each person has a spirit, a soul. Unless you are a truly evil person (think incest, human sacrifice) your soul lives forever. There is room for every Jewish soul in Paradise. If you develop your soul (by studying and following the laws of the Torah), you get a big portion of Paradise. It's a deal you can't pass up.

Another rarely discussed topic is reincarnation. Believe it or not, reincarnation is entirely possible. If a great soul has something left to accomplish on Earth, it will be reborn into another body. This is an Orthodox concept. More-modern movements do not tout reincarnation.

TIMING

The Book of Genesis (3:19) says, "For dust thou art, and unto dust shalt thou return." According to Jewish law, the body must be buried within twenty-four hours unless the Sabbath or a Holy Day intervenes. A quick burial shows respect for the recently departed and moves the grieving process along for the survivors. While the burial must be postponed for the Sabbath and major holidays and festivals, it can be delayed for:

✡ Government paperwork
✡ Postmortem examinations but not autopsies—Judaism is against mutilating the corpse
✡ Delivery of shrouds and caskets
✡ Close relatives traveling from great distances
✡ Availability of rabbi of choice

Jews believe that in death, you are absolved of all sins and go on to live forever in God's kingdom, as exemplified by the prayer one says when dying, excerpted from a prayer book:

May my death be an atonement for whatever sins and errors and wrongdoings I have committed before Thee. In Thy mercy grant me of the goodness that is waiting for the righteous, and bring me to eternal life.

JUDGMENT DAY

" *Three women die in a car crash: a Protestant, a Catholic, and a Jew. They show up at the gates of Heaven. The gatekeeper first greets the Protestant. "Mrs. Smith, you have led a good life. Please go up the stairs and to the right."*

He addressed the Catholic woman next. "Mrs. O'Neil, you have been a good mother and an upstanding member of the community. Welcome to Heaven. Please go up the stairs and to the right."

Finally, he turns to the Jew. "Ah, Mrs. Abramowitz, you have been a kind and loving person. Please go upstairs and to the left."

Mrs. Abramowitz hesitates and says, "Hey, how come my friends get to go to the right and I have to go to the left? Don't I get to go to Heaven? "

The gatekeeper says, "I thought you'd like to get your hair done first." "

LOCATION

Thanks to a change of venue, going to funerals is much better than it used to be. Memorial services used to take place before the funeral in either the home of the deceased or at the cemetery. Now there are scores of Jewish funeral homes.

SERVICE

The funeral service is mercifully short and simple, and takes place at the gravesite. It focuses on honoring the dead not comforting the mourners. Until the burial, all attention is directed at the dearly departed. Thanks to the quick interment and short service, the burial doesn't take very long and people can quickly get back to worrying about themselves.

BURIAL

Jewish law forbids any displays or ostentation, like large bouquets of flowers, at the funeral. The coffin should be a simple wooden box with no metal on it in order to facilitate the decomposition process. The body is wrapped in a white sheet, or kittel, rather than being clothed. As death comes equally to all people, all people should come equally to death.

Jews don't do open caskets or visitations. We don't like to dress up our dead. It's creepy. It doesn't bring closure. It's not doing the deceased any favors. This is important to keep in mind if your Jewish partner accompanies you to a Catholic wake. Since chances are a Jew would not expect to see a body, you'll know why your partner has broken into a cold sweat in front of the casket. Do him or her a favor and give a little warning.

Cremation is not acceptable among Orthodox Jews because it doesn't show respect to the body God created. Reform Jews allow it but it isn't done that often. Burying the dead is a mitzvah (commandment). If you cremate, you can't perform this mitzvah. Also, it is mutilation of the corpse, which Judaism is against. The human body is a holy vessel, after all. Treat it with respect.

TEAR IT UP

Before the funeral, members of the family of the deceased pin a small torn black ribbon on their clothes. The ribbon remains there for the entire week of mourning, called shivah.

Originally, mourners actually ripped their clothes to show that a loved one has been torn from the fabric of their lives. Orthodox Jews still tear their clothes. The act of tearing provides a way for the survivors to release some of the anger they may feel over the death in a religiously sanctioned manner.

In Orthodox tradition, everyone over the age of thirteen in the immediate family of the deceased tears a small section of their outer garment (vest, jacket, or sweater). In-laws and divorced mates can rip their garments as well if they sincerely want to, but not if it offends their own living parents. The following are not supposed to tear their clothes: bride and groom within first seven days of marriage, the mentally ill, the physically handicapped, or those too weak to make the tear themselves. After the mourning period, the tear can be sewn. For the sake of modesty, daughters can sew their clothes immediately after the funeral. Everyone else wears the rip for thirty days. For Conservative and Reform Jews, the torn ribbon is an accepted symbolic substitute.

The whole pallbearer thing is pretty much the same as in Christianity. The only difference is that the pallbearers must be Jewish. Friends or family of the deceased carry the coffin to the grave. However, Orthodox and Conservative men descending from the Kohen tribe* cannot serve as pallbearers.

After the coffin is lowered into the grave, it is immediately covered with handfuls of dirt by the deceased's spouse and children. Then other relatives throw dirt onto the coffin. The rest of the job is finished by the other mourners at the gravesite or, in less religious

---

*The Kohanim (plural for Kohen, also Cohen, Cohn, Kahn) are descendants of Aaron, Moses' brother and the first high priest of the Tabernacle (a tent sanctuary used by the Israelites during the Exodus) in biblical times. As descendants of the priestly tribe, throughout the ages, Kohanim have been given certain honorary roles in religious ritual. One of the restrictions still observed is that a male Kohen may not set foot in a cemetery except for the burial of his closest relatives.

In a nutshell: Burial is for the dead. Mourning is for the living.

families, by the cemetery workers. The grave is filled in before the family leaves to give them a sense of completion.

The headstone should be simple yet of high quality so as to last for many years. It is not placed on the grave immediately but sometime within a year after the burial. It usually happens about eleven months after the death to mark the end of the required mourning period. There is a very brief and simple ceremony, called the "unveiling." A psalm is read, a few comforting words are said, and then the deceased's spouse, children, or closest relatives remove the cover that until this moment hid the inscription. They say two prayers, the Kaddish (pronounced "KAH-dish") and the El Maleh Rahamim ("el-mah-leh rah-ha-meem").

When visiting a gravesite, place a pebble or small stone on the headstone rather than flowers to show that you were there. Jews also don't usually plant shrubs or flowers on graves. This is in keeping with the tradition of a simple burial. Planting things at gravesites, the rabbis believed, could lead to competition for the biggest and the best. What? The Jews competitive?

THE FIVE STAGES OF MOURNING

Mourning is definitely a process for Jews. There are five distinct stages. The first, the time between death and burial, is the shortest but most intense. The grief is strong but arrangements need to be made. There isn't much time to focus on sorrow. Weeping and lamentation is postponed until the second period, the three days following the funeral.

The third period, the seven days after the burial, overlaps with the second period. This period is called shivah, the Hebrew word for seven. During this period, the family does not leave the house. They stay at home and receive visitors every evening for seven days. It used to be that people would wait to pay condolences until the fourth day after the funeral. Before that the family was supposed to be too overcome with grief to receive visitors. Today there is no time for that. Many families have reduced the shivah period to a few days after the funeral. Most come to pay their condolences right after the funeral. Most families, however, still burn a large white memorial candle for the full seven days.

LIMITS FOR STAGES OF GRIEVING SET BY THE TORAH

Weeping, three days

Lamenting, seven days

Ignoring personal appearance, thirty days

The shivah is the time to give your condolences. Don't try to comfort a mourner before the burial. Wait until after the funeral. Until the burial, all attention should be on the dead.

When going directly from the funeral to the shivah house, custom calls for mourners to wash their hands before entering the house. By doing this, mourners are washing off "death," which they may have carried with them from the funeral. They can also wash off any dirt from the gravesite.

In a Jewish house of mourning, all mirrors are covered with cloth. Originally, this was done because people did not want the spirit of death, hovering over the home of the deceased, to see its own reflection in the mirror and take up residence in the house. Today, it is explained by saying that people in a house of mourning should not be vain.

Members of the immediate family also remove their shoes upon entering the house and sit on low stools, benches, or even boxes—a custom derived from ancient mourning rituals. We don't need to be so comfortable when one of our own has just passed.

As mentioned before, Judaism concentrates on life, and even in mourning people are expected to go on with their lives. Family and friends at a shivah house will laugh and cry together, remembering the deceased with love. Photos and stories come out as mourners reminisce about those who are gone.

Daily, a minyan (ten bar mitzvah'd men) must form in the shivah home so family members can say the Kaddish, or mourner's prayer. The Kaddish is spoken in Aramaic rather than in Hebrew. Oddly enough, the prayer contains no direct reference to death or to the deceased. It is a prayer that speaks of faith in God's rulings and the wish for the coming of the Messiah.

Seeing what has happened to the length of the shivah, it will be no surprise to hear the fourth and fifth stages of mourning are generally ignored by all but the Orthodox. Still, it's the tradition and you should know about it. The fourth stage is called *sheloshim*, which means thirty in Hebrew, and it lasts for the thirty days following the funeral. The mourner is encouraged to leave the house after seven days at home and begin to return to the community. Torn clothes or black ribbons are still worn, however, and the mourner is not sup-

WHEN IN MOURNING A JEW SHOULD

Sit shivah, seven days

Sit on low stools or boxes, seven days

Wear slippers, seven days

Say Kaddish every day, eleven months when mourning a parent

WHEN IN MOURNING A JEW SHOULD NOT

Shave, thirty days

Wear makeup, seven days

Have sex, seven days

Buy new clothes, thirty days

Study anything but biblical volumes on grief, seven days

Keep a normal work schedule, seven days

Attend parties, concerts, or entertainment, eleven months when mourning a parent

JEWISH LEGACY: THE ETHICAL WILL

This supplement to the last will and testament is a parent's attempt to leave moral guidelines for their children after they are gone. Leave it to Jewish parents to try to run their kids' lives from the grave.

• • • • • • • • • • • • • • • • • • • •

posed to cut his hair or shave. He also cannot go to anything festive or celebratory. Parties are out for the final period as well. This fifth stage lasts for the eleven months after the funeral. Sons of the deceased say Kaddish every day, avoid entertainment, but otherwise go about life as usual.

PAYING RESPECTS TO THE DEAD

Do not send flowers to the deceased's family or funeral home. In ancient times, mourners used flowers to help mask the odor of the decaying body. Thankfully, this is no longer necessary. Rather than sending pricey floral monstrosities, Jews show their respect for the deceased by making a donation. A family will often request that donations be sent to their temple, a Jewish hospital, or a favorite charity. Another suggestion is to have a tree planted in Israel.

COMFORTING THE MOURNERS

Food, as you've already seen, is an integral part of Jewish life. Just as families gather around dinner tables in festive times, Jews console each other with food as well. Traditional Jewish foods such as kugel, knishes, bagels and lox, and hard-boiled eggs (symbolic of the need for life to go on) are often served at the shivah house for mourning guests. In addition, guests are expected to bring dishes so the family doesn't have to worry about cooking. In fact, there is a chance that those in mourning will not remember to eat. As eating means to continue living, others ensure this by bringing food. Fruit baskets and baked goods are always a safe bet.

Don't pack a to-go bag. Judy Mass found this out when she brought leftover kugel (You can't waste good kugel!) from a shivah house to a Yom Kippur Break the Fast. Her friend Elaine whispered loudly, "You *never* take food from a shivah house."

REMEMBERING THE DEARLY DEPARTED

A son is supposed to say Kaddish for eleven months following the death of a parent. He should say the Kaddish every day or at least when in temple on the Sabbath. Daughters can say it but it's frowned upon by the Orthodox. It is not optional for a son. It is his duty. If there are no sons, another can say Kaddish for the deceased but not if his own parents are alive.

This is one of the few prayers that must be said in community. So in order to fulfill this mitzvah, the mourner must go to temple. While it can be inconvenient to haul it to temple every day, being around others while grieving is reported to be very therapeutic.

Reciting the Kaddish is a mitzvah. One who says Kaddish is doing a good thing for both themselves and the deceased. Praising God is good to do for the strengthening of one's own soul. Saying Kaddish also accepts God's putting an end to the parent's life. More important, it merits the soul of the departed. They are the reason why the mourner is praising God and that helps their immortal soul.

On the *yahrtzeit,* or the anniversary of the death, family members light a memorial candle that burns for a little over twenty-four hours and say the Kaddish. Survivors also light the yahrtzcit candle in memoriam on Yom Kippur.

The Mourner's Kaddish

"May His great Name be exalted and sanctified in the world He created according to his will; And may He establish His Kingship during your lifetime and during your days and during the lifetime of the entire family of Israel, swiftly and soon. May His great Name be blessed forever and ever. Blessed, lauded, glorified, extolled, upraised, honored, elevated, and praised be the name of the Holy One, blessed be He, beyond all blessings, songs, praises, and consolations that are uttered on Earth. May there be abundant peace from Heaven, and life upon us and upon all Israel. He who makes peace in His heights, may He make peace upon us, and upon all Israel."

EUTHANASIA

Jewish law condemns cutting off the life of a person even by just minutes. Modern rabbis, however, will allow a terminally ill patient to take pain-limiting drugs even if a side effect is shortening his life. They also believe that a terminal patient should not be kept alive on artificial life-sustaining devices but should be allowed to die in dignity.

"I don't want to achieve immortality through my work; I want to achieve immortality through not dying."

—WOODY ALLEN (1935–)

Several times a year, temples hold memorial services, called *Yizkor* (yits-kor). This includes passages from the Torah and special prayers as well as silent reflection. The service also remembers those who died for the sanctification of God's name, and some have a special prayer for the 6 million Jews who perished in the Holocaust. Jews also remember those who have died by naming their children in honor and in memory.

When talking about the departed, you should frequently throw in the term *"alav hashalom"* (pronounced "ah-lav ha-shah-lome"), meaning "may he rest in peace." For example, "My grandfather on my dad's side, *alav hashalom*, was a very fat man. My other grandfather, *alav hashalom*, was a very rich man."

SUICIDE

Jews don't believe in suicide. Jews strive to survive. They abhor suicide for several reasons. It is disrespectful to kill the image of God. (This means any person, yourself included, since man was made in the image of God.) A suicide also deprives the family of their presence. If an adult commits suicide, there is no shivah and family members do not tear their clothes. Friends and community, however, will still line up to console the family. Anything done is done for the family not for the deceased. In actuality, Jews rarely rule it suicide when someone kills himself. Instead, they say it was an accident or temporary insanity to avoid putting the stigma of suicide on the bereaved family.

There are special occasions when Judaism permits suicide: when death is certain anyway, and when life would be a shameful existence. Both of these reasons came into play when 960 Jews killed themselves and their families at Masada (on the west shore of the Dead Sea) in C.E. 73. The Romans were approaching their fortress and they chose a mass suicide rather than be killed or taken into slavery.

Epilogue

So, you finished the book! Mazel tov! (If you don't know what that means, go back to Chapter 4 immediately.) We're sure you've learned a few things along the way—at least enough to get by gracefully and comfortably in Jewish circles.

What to Do When You're Dating a Jew was meant to cover the basics of Judaism and give you a better understanding of what your friends and loved ones are all about. You may find that there are still some aspects of the religion or culture you'd like to learn more about. The books and movies we've listed at the back of the book will provide additional insight.

If you read or see something you didn't agree with or made you uncomfortable, discuss it with your partner. An open dialogue is what's important. If nothing else, this book will give you much to talk about. And Jews love to talk.

Shalom!

Sources for Future Study

You still want more? All right, more you shall have. Continue with your exploration of the Jewish culture with the resources listed here.

MOVIES

A Price Above Rubies (1998): A look inside the Orthodox community.

Annie Hall (1977): A romance between the always neurotic Woody and his non-Jewish girlfriend played by Diane Keaton. Or any other Woody Allen movie should suffice.

Au Revoir Les Enfants (1987): French Catholic boarding school takes in a Jewish student during World War II. Director Louis Malle based the film on his experiences.

Avalon (1990): Director Barry Levinson tells about his immigrant family's experiences in Baltimore at the beginning of the century.

Ben-Hur (1959): Charlton Heston plays the Jewish prince who is sent into slavery by a Roman friend (some friend!) and later gets revenge.

Brighton Beach Memoirs (1986) and any Neil Simon film: Eugene, a Jewish teenager, recalls living with his extended family in the forties and fifties.

Crossing Delancey (1988): A New York bookseller, a pickle man, and an old-fashioned Jewish matchmaker.

Fiddler on the Roof (1971): Russian peasant Tevye copes with the day-to-day problems of tradition, his family, and state-sanctioned pogroms.

Goodbye, Columbus (1969): Based on Philip Roth's book about a difficult romance between a working-class Jewish man (Richard Benjamin) and his Jewish American Princess girlfriend, played (ironically) by Ali MacGraw.

Hester Street (1975): Jewish immigrants in late nineteenth century New York struggle to create a balance between assimilating and preserving their culture and traditions.

Jakob the Liar (1999): Robin Williams plays a Jewish café owner who tries to keep hope alive in Nazi-occupied Poland.

Marjorie Morningstar (1958): Natalie Wood and Gene Kelly star in this film about an unlikely romance between Marjorie Morgenstern and a non-Jewish second-rate composer. Book by Herman Wouk.

Private Benjamin (1980): Goldie Hawn is a Jewish American Princess who joins the army on a whim. Great Jewish wedding scene.

Schindler's List (1993): Steven Spielberg directed this masterpiece about a factory owner who protects his Jewish workers during the Nazi occupation. Starring Liam Neeson, Ralph Fiennes, Embeth Davidtz, and Ben Kingsley.

Sophie's Choice (1982): Sophie (Meryl Streep) is a survivor of a Nazi concentration camp with a dark secret. Also starring Kevin Kline.

The Chosen (1981): In 1940s New York, a friendship between an Orthodox Jew (Robby Benson) and a Reform Jew weathers their differences.

The Ten Commandments (1956): Don't miss this classic.

Yentl (1983): A woman (Barbra Streisand) breaks with tradition to study the Torah.

BOOKS

Publishing information for these titles can be found in the bibliography.

The Nine Questions People Ask About Judaism by Dennis Prager and Joseph Telushkin.

This Is My God by Herman Wouk

The Search for God at Harvard by Ari L. Goldman

A Jew Today by Elie Wiesel

The Diary of Anne Frank

Bet You Didn't Know

FAMOUS JEWS (. . . OR SO WE HEAR)

Aaron and Tori Spelling, producer and actress

Adam Duritz, lead singer/songwriter for
  Counting Crows

Adam Sandler, comedian

Alan Dershowitz, lawyer, writer

Albert Brooks, actor, director—real name:
  Albert Einstein

Albert Einstein, physicist

Alicia Silverstone, actress

Annie Leibovitz, photographer

Barbara Boxer, senator from California

Barbara Hershey, actress—real name:
  Herzstein

Barbra Streisand, singer, actress, director

Ben and Jerry Stiller, actor/director and actor

Bette Midler, singer, actress

Betty Friedan, feminist, author

Billy Crystal, actor, comedian

Bob Dylan, musician

Buzz Aldrin, astronaut

Calvin Klein, fashion designer

Camille Pisarro, artist

Carly Simon, singer

Coen Brothers, directors

David Copperfield, magician

David Geffen, producer, record label owner

David Schwimmer, actor

Dr. Laura Schessinger, radio personality

Dr. Ruth Westheimer, sex therapist

Dr. (Theodore) Seuss (Geisel), author

Ed Koch, former Mayor of New York

Fran Lebowitz, writer

Fred Astaire, dancer—real name: Frederik
  Austerlitz

George Burns, comedian—real name: Nathan
  Birnbaum

George Gershwin, composer

Gertrude Stein, writer

Gilda Radner, comedienne

Goldie Hawn, actress

Gwyneth Paltrow, actress

Harry Houdini, magician—real name: Ehrich Weiss

Henry Kissinger, former U.S. secretary of state

Henry Winkler, actor

Irving Berlin, composer—real name: Israel Baline

Isaac Asimov, writer

Jeff Goldblum, actor

Jeffrey Katzenberg, producer

Jerry Seinfeld, comedian

Joan Rivers, comedienne

Jonas Salk, inventor of polio vaccine

Joyce Brothers, psychologist

Judge Judy, TV judge

Judy Blume, author

Karl Marx, philosopher

Kirk and Mike Douglas, actors

Lauren Bacall, actress—real name: Betty Joan Perske

Lenny Bruce, comedian

Leonard Nemoy, actor

Lisa Kudrow, actress

Marc Chagall, painter

Marx Brothers, comedians

Matt Stone, cocreator of "South Park"

Maurice Sendak, writer

Melissa Gilbert, actress

Michael Eisner, businessman

Michael Landon, actor, director—real name: Eugene Orowitz

Mickey Cohen, gangster

Natalie Portman, actress

Neil Diamond, singer, actor

Neil Simon, director

Noah Wyle, actor

Nora Ephron, writer, director

Paul Allen, Microsoft founder

Paul Reiser, actor, comedian

Peter Max, artist

Ralph Lauren, clothes designer—real name: Ralph Lipshitz

Richard Dreyfuss, actor

Roy Lichtenstein, painter

Ruth Bader Ginsberg, U.S. Supreme Court justice

Sammy Davis Jr., singer

Sandy Koufax, baseball player

Sarah Jessica Parker, actress

Shel Silverstein, writer

Sigmund Freud, psychotherapist

Simon and Garfunkel, singers

Stanley Kaplan, founder of college preparatory courses

Stanley Kubrick, director of *2001, A Clockwork Orange, The Shining,* among others

Steven Spielberg, director

Tara Lipinski, women's world figure skating champion, 1997; gold medalist 1998 Olympic Games

Tony Curtis, actor—real name: Bernard Schwartz

Vidal Sassoon, a member of the early Israeli government

William Shatner, actor

Woody Allen, writer, actor, director—real name: Allen Konigsberg

MECCAS OF AMERICAN JEWRY

PRE-1970s

Bronx, Brooklyn, Queens, Manhattan, Long
Island, New York
Hyde Park (Chicago), Illinois
Skokie, Illinois
Miami, Florida
Los Angeles, California

POST-1970s:

Newton/Brookline, Massachusetts
New York City
Northern New Jersey
Highland Park, Illinois
Boca Raton, Florida
Palm Beach, Florida

FACTOID

In the United States, the largest Jewish population is in New York; the smallest Jewish population
is in Wyoming.

Bibliography

Aleichem, Sholem. *Tevye the Dairyman and the Railroad Stories.* New York: Schocken Books Inc., 1987.

Bridger, David, ed. *The New Jewish Encyclopedia;* New York: Behrman House, Inc., 1962.

Casey, Betty. *International Folk Dancing U.S.A.* Garden City, N.Y.: Doubleday & Company, Inc., 1981.

Emmes, Yetta. *Drek! The Real Yiddish Your Bubbe Never Taught You.* New York: Penguin Publishing, Inc., 1998.

Feldman, David M. *Birth Control in Jewish Law.* New York: New York University Press, 1968.

Frank, Anne. *Anne Frank: The Diary of a Young Girl.* New York: Doubleday, 1987.

Goldman, Ari L. *The Search for God at Harvard.* New York: Ballantine Books, 1991.

Greene, Hank. *Square and Folk Dancing.* New York: Harper & Row, 1984.

Gross, David C. *Dictionary of 1000 Jewish Proverbs.* New York: Hippocrene Books, Inc., 1997.

———. *1,201 Questions and Answers About Judaism.* New York: Hippocrene Books, Inc., 1987.

Hoffman, Paul, and Matt Freedman. *Dictionary Shmictionary!* New York: William Morrow, 1983.

Lamm, Maurice. *The Jewish Way in Death and Mourning.* New York: Jonathan David Publishers, Inc., 1969.

Menchin, Robert. *101 Classic Jewish Jokes: Jewish Humor from Groucho Marx to Jerry Seinfeld.* Memphis, Tenn.: Mustang Publishing, 1998.

Novak, William, and Moshe Waldoks. *The Big Book of Jewish Humor.* New York: HarperCollins, 1981.

Prager, Dennis, and Joseph Telushkin. *The Nine Questions People Ask About Judaism.* New York: Simon & Schuster, 1975.

Schermann, Nosson, and Meir Zlotowitz, eds. *Kaddish—Expositions on Jewish Liturgy and Thought.* New York: Mesorah Publications, Ltd., 1980.

Spalding, Henry D., ed. *Encyclopedia of Jewish Humor.* New York: Jonathan David Publishers, 1969.

Swarner, Kristina, illus. *Yiddish Wisdom.* San Francisco: Chronicle Books, 1996.

Telushkin, Rabbi Joseph. *Jewish Wisdom: Ethical, Spiritual, and Historical Lessons from the Great Works and Thinkers.* New York: William Morrow, 1994.

Wiesel, Elie. *A Jew Today.* New York: Vintage Books, 1978.

Wouk, Herman. *This Is My God.* Boston: Little Brown and Company, 1959.

Index